Dear Bully

DEDICATION	2
INTRODUCTION	2
ACKNOWLEDGEMENTS	5
THE BOOK BREAKDOWN	6
ELEMENTARY SCHOOL	8
Chapter 1: Learning Disability	11
Chapter 2: In-Family Bullying	12
Chapter 3: Abusive Home	15
Chapter 4: Snitching Culture	17
Chapter 5: Apologies Wanted and No Room for Forgiveness	19
Chapter 6: Sibling Bullying Cycle	22
Chapter 7: Roasting and Teasing	25
Chapter 8: Racial Bullying, Stereotypes, and Language Barriers	28
Chapter 9: Cyberbullying/Online Safety	34
Chapter 10: The Power of Positive Affirmations	36
Chapter 11: Parent Divorce and Summer Camp	41
Chapter 12: Conflict Resolution for Hitting Behaviors	44
Chapter 13: New Kid-New School Drama	47
MIDDLE AND HIGH SCHOOL	54
Chapter 14: Stress and Anxiety and Bullying	60
Chapter 15: Teasing and Roasting	63
Chapter 16: Friendship Drama	68
Chapter 17: Toxic Friendships and Exclusion	75
Chapter 18: Toxic Romantic Relationships	86
Chapter 19: Self-Esteem Thermometer	90
Chapter 20: The Cycle of Bullying	104
Chapter 21: Slut-Shaming	114
Chapter 22: Sexual Identity and Sexual Orientation	120

Dedication

I dedicate this book to my late brother Jason Peagram. He is my reason for doing this work with youth, to try to eliminate bullying and violence in schools. I lost him to gun violence almost ten years ago. That somber day, my life changed forever. My work is dedicated to him. If I can keep one child from pulling a gun on another kid and I get to save those two irreplaceable lives, then I know I am exactly where I am supposed to be. I want his legacy to live on through Bulldog. I want his story to be known.

Introduction

This book is the first of a series. Over the last ten years, Bulldog Solution has worked in the education field. We run various programs where we help children and teens let go of the pain of bullying. These programs include bullying prevention assemblies, student SEL programs, advisory train-the-trainer workshops, professional development for teachers, and parent meetings. In our Dear Bully assemblies and our 8-week Peace Over Drama (POD) program, we collect letters of forgiveness and apology between students to help with the healing process.

This book is a compilation of these letters, where children and teens share their emotions, behaviors, and thoughts around bullying and drama. These are their stories—raw, real, and for us to understand. Some stories will rip you straight through the heart; others might disturb you or leave you unsettled. That is the world we live in. Privilege and power often override kindness and compassion. We are so busy checking our followers and updating our stories on social media that we often forget to look across the table at the people who matter most to us. Suicide, depression, and anxiety are at all-time highs. I don't need any statistics or research to tell me that; I see it every day in the schools and corporations where I work. I see people's pain, their anger, their despair, but I believe that there is hope.

This book is not a revolutionary answer, or magical solution, but more a manual for getting back to being kind and considerate. We must put ourselves in the other person's shoes and understand that our emotions have a lot of impact on our thoughts and behaviors. We have to learn to feel and process our emotions, so we can heal, de-stress, and be in the moment. Only by being present (physically and mentally), building connections, listening to one another, and being kind, will we eradicate bullying. Hating on each other, yelling at each other, and dismissing each other do not do us justice. We live in an era of fear, and fear fuels hate, resentment, and anger. Demanding respect by belittling people as we say is not a solution for eradicating bullying. Instead, those behaviors fuel bullying. Punishing causes more resentment and anger; it does not stop bullying. We need to understand the root cause of bullying and use kindness as our weapon against it. Kindness is the most powerful weapon, and it is my ammunition of choice.

My name is Dr. Kortney Peagram, and I am a Bully Teacher. I am a born French Canadian who nested here in Chicago seventeen years ago. I am also the founder and the dreamer of Bulldog Solution. I created this company, and I have poured my heart into what I have built over the past ten years. I have one dream; I have one passion; and I have one mission: the eradication of bullying through kindness, connection, and social boldness. My one legacy will be to have left this world knowing that I did my best to fight the epidemic of bullying by fueling kindness. My mantra is Kindness Always Wins. I challenge you to read on and better understand these stories. You might be surprised about you how you can relate, or maybe some memories will emerge, and you will identify with the person writing the letter.

In building this company, I learned many hard lessons. I have met some mean people; I have been bullied, ridiculed, and shunned in my own industry. My job is not all sunshine and roses; it can be dark and challenging to work in this field. There have been instances where I walked out of a school and beelined it to my car to cry or scream my head off. I have had staff walk off programs, get punched, kicked, and pushed. I have had to console staff who were so perturbed by a program that they thought they were in the wrong line of work.

At Bulldog, we call those instances getting "rocked."—when we lead a program and realize that the group is running us. In that moment, we know everything is about to go downhill. The situation might get nasty, hairy, and quite uncomfortable. It is the equivalent of getting our ass kicked then handed back to us. In those moments, we say, "Thank you; I still have a ton to learn."

Our hardest programs are the ones where the children are hurting the most. They have built walls of resistance to hide from their trauma. These children can be vicious and can target our weaknesses. They sabotage our activities or simply tell us to f*ck off. In those programs, I put on my big girl pants, scrape up all my courage, and sit with kindness until I get a breakthrough. Sometimes, it takes a long time, and sometimes it never happens. I do hope that one day, the children will think back about our experience and know that they are loved and supported. I hope that I have at least planted a seed or ruffled a feather to get them to see things slightly differently. Most of the time, we never know the impact we have had, but at other times, we get to see our children blossom into incredible leaders.

This work at times is extremely difficult; I have experienced multiple burnouts, compassion fatigue, and have been emotionally drained. I have been numbed to a certain amount of violence and difficult behaviors. I have been challenged almost to a point of no return.

However, when the sun rises after the storm, when the dust settles after the pain, and I can see the fruits of our labor, I know without a doubt that this work is meant for me. No matter how hard this work gets, the moments of love and kindness trump everything. I absolutely love my work. If I had unlimited resources and could do anything I wanted, I would still choose Bulldog. The *why* is what keeps me going. Over the years, I have been moved by children's kindness, touched by teachers' support and care, and inspired by principals' desire to change the educational system.

On my darkest days, when I can't seem to catch a break, there is always a sign that I am exactly where I am supposed to be. I often ask the Universe for a sign, and it gives me one. The sign might be a letter, an email, someone stopping me on the street, a note on my

Facebook page, or a parent calling me to say thank you. Just sharing that with you brings me tears of joy. I love the small miracles that happen in my work. The small gestures create the most impact.

I have collected letters from children dating back almost eight years—letters of gratitude, sharing how their time with Bulldog saved their lives; emails from students saying that they are studying social work or psychology because they want to help people; words about how much they gained from our programs. Those are my ticker; they are my motivation; they are what keeps me going—the lives we save, the children we serve. The journey we embark on as Bully Teachers is the most rewarding experience. It is a wild ride, and I am thrilled to share my world with you. These stories are meant for us to connect to each other and seek a better understanding of who we are at the core.

To write this book, I used what I like to call the "power of three." My two co-authors have worked with me, have worked with students, and have worked to bring this book to life. Their names are Shannon Edwards and Alexandra Zimmerman.

Shannon Edwards is a soon-to-be graduate of a master's degree in psychology. She is a biracial individual (half black, half white) who moved to Chicago over a year ago from Pennsylvania, where she grew up in a predominantly white town. Shannon feels that being biracial is a big part of her identity, as she has had to navigate our world using two lenses. She was a varsity athlete and understands team and leadership dynamics. She thrives in groups and really brings life to our programs. She is a straight shooter and will call out any child who is being disrespectful. She is fast and witty. She is young and vibrant. She brings light and fun to our team. Although she admits to never having been bullied, she does recognize times in her life where she felt exclusion and discrimination. She relates best to teens, mostly angry teens, and she has a magical power to turn them around to be kinder humans. She is constantly working on herself and learning. She strives to improve and take on new adventures. Her mission is to develop herself and to help others discover their true power. She is a big advocate for building trust and emotional intelligence. Shannon dedicates this book to her mom and dad, the people who made her a strong, confident, brave, driven, and fun-loving person.

Alexandra Zimmerman, M.A. is a recent graduate of The Chicago School of Professional Psychology. She grew up in Chicago, has lived there all of her life, and is a strong Latina. Alexandra is passionate about protecting our children and educating them about emotional intelligence and empathy. She is the easiest person to talk to. She is relatable, engaging, fun, and positive. She enters a room and brings with her a bundle of positivity and energy. She makes you feel like you are the most incredible person. She listens and relates to young women so well. She has helped a ton of teenage girls in our groups. She sits with them and is their biggest advocate. She really loves working to help them see their inner beauty. Alexandra remembers being young and how hurtful and painful it was to be bullied in school. She wishes that no other child would go through such pain. She works hard to build girls' self-esteem. She shows up for the girls when they need her. Alexandra's mission is to help people understand the importance of empathy and kindness. By being kind, you can make a large impact on the world. As a new mom, Alexandra wants to help create a kinder world for her daughter and all children. She dedicates this book to her beautiful daughter Josie.

Our different experiences, ethnicity, and generational backgrounds have made us relatable to the students with whom we work in our programs. The power of three brings our voices together as we respond to some of the letters in this book. We collected these letters throughout the process of running our Dear Bully assemblies, and we sometimes responded to them. As you will notice, we have different writing patterns, and you might recognize which Bully Teacher responded to the letter. However, as we brought this book to life, we decided to be united as one. In the letters and the responses we have collected to use in this book, we have eliminated our individual names and chosen to sign our letters as The Bully Teacher. We bring our voices together; together we make a difference.

In closing, I leave you with this thought: There is not one child who is born into this world with hate. There is not one child who wakes up one day and thinks to themselves, "I am going to bully." It is a learned behavior; it is simply a product of their environment. People who bully are not tough, strong, or confident. They are in pain, sad, angry, alone, and weak. They use their power to inflict pain, so they don't feel so alone. Their behavior is not right or fair, but it is what is happening.

Here are the stories, here are the anecdotes, here are the tales of our life as a Bully Teacher.

Sending you love and positivity on this wild journey of life,

The Bully Teacher
Dr. Kortney Peagram

Acknowledgements

I have had the help of my team for this book, and I am grateful for the work they have put into it. Shannon Edwards and Alexandra Zimmerman are co-authors. They helped with the responses, they sat with the kids, and they share their stories. Michael Althouse did all the transcribing and edited along the way. He spent nearly three years working with teens and children. He was an incredible addition and value to our team. Without them and all of the other members of Bulldog Solution, this book would not have been possible.

The Book Breakdown

We worked on this book for over a year, but we have collected these stories for over ten years. This is the first book of a series. The idea of this book is to provide a better understanding of the trends that we see in our schools. Our goal is for parents and educators to gain knowledge and extract strategies and tips to use for the children in their lives, at whatever stage those children are. We have broken the book down in a few different ways.

At the beginning of each chapter, we have created an "Area of Focus," which addresses the common behaviors, emotions, and attitudes that students often experience during this time in their lives.

After the Area of Focus are the letters. Typically, we collect these letters halfway through our program; by this time, our students are better at understanding emotions, sharing experiences, and processing social interactions. At other times, students write to us in their journals, and we can see shifts in their attitudes or behaviors over time. We have changed all identifiers except grade levels and gender. We have been able to match some of the letters to their recipients. For others, we decided to share our perspectives and strategies as The Bully Teacher. We collected all of these stories from children who have participated in our programs, so a pattern emerges of apologies or students clarifying their emotions as they apply their learning right into the letters.

This book is divided into two sections: "elementary school" and "middle and high school." Elementary school stands alone, because the stories are more general, as they tend to be in this age group. Most of the letters from this age group revolve around simple-to-understand conflicts—teasing, exclusion, family dynamics, etc. As we move to middle school and high school, we begin to see similar issues emerge, to different extents. Peer pressure, complex relationships, trauma, and self-identity trouble increase in these grades. The complexity of the issues in the letter is based not so much on the students' grade level but more on the students' maturity, cognitive ability, emotional intelligence, socioeconomic background, and demographic.

After some of the letters we have sometimes included updates or additional responses to add clarity. Sometimes a child wrote a letter to a bully, and we felt a strong need to respond and get them the help they needed to heal. We want to provide the clearest understanding of each scenario.

The "Stop & Think" sections are designed to explain the situation better and to provide insight about how to address bullying or drama situations. We added a great deal of content to the "Stop and Think" section to provide examples, sample narratives, and ideas to use with children. We also talk about the "Do and Don't" actions. We share more about how children perceive themselves and how to increase their social and emotional wellness at home. You may not agree with some of the strategies , and we respect that. We want to share what we do and what we have seen in schools. It is a take on our perspective.

At the end of each chapter, the reader will find a "Reflection Checkpoint," a section that reviews the main points from the "Stop and Think" and provides some food for thought and additional ideas that might be helpful.

To recap, the book is broken down as follows:
1. Area of Focus: These are trends we see within that grade.
2. Definitions to Know: We include important terms and keywords to know.
3. Letters: They will start with a "Dear Bully," "Dear Victim," or "Dear Bulldog."
4. Updates: We include updates to shed light on an incident or provide additional notes about a letter.
5. Stop and Think: This section is a breakdown of behaviors and helpful tips or narratives for how to address more complex situations.
6. Reflection Checkpoint: This is a recap of the most important points.

Throughout the book, we define and clarify different definitions or terms. The definitions help us explain behaviors and identify the best strategy for addressing them. At the end of the book is a list of references for the few times we have used research or a theory or model. This book is not intended for research purposes. It is intended to bring clarity and a better understanding of what is going in our schools.

Elementary School

Area of Focus

We collected the following stories from a wide range of elementary schools. Often, in early elementary, students struggle with making friends and expanding their group of friends. There are a lot of exclusions and drama. Kids telling their friends that they can only be friends with one person or that they can't talk to a certain classmate. These exclusions are part of their development in learning about boundaries and understanding social dynamics. It is important to step in to mediate these situations, explaining *why* it is important for them to open their circle of friends at a young age and to be kind to their classmates. Children need more direction about how to interact with each other. Often, they don't know how to make friends, introduce themselves, or resolve conflict, so they revert to what they know, and their behavior turns into drama or bullying.

Going over how to make friends is critical in early elementary. We find that more and more children don't know how to make introductions to new children or how to ask to play with each other. If students are more energetic or forceful, they can be seen as bullies. When students are quieter and keep to themselves, they might be seen as aloof or unapproachable. By learning more about group dynamics and practicing how to teach children to be friends and communicate, we can eliminate early signs of drama and bullying. In elementary school, we see a lot of in-family bullying (sibling bullying), friendship drama, hitting behaviors, and anger outbursts. These behaviors are typical, and we want to provide you with resources to help make this behavior atypical.

In elementary school, children are learning how to express their emotions, and often, if they feel big emotions, they might struggle to express themselves and might resort to aggressive tendencies. For these children, the next best thing to expressing their emotions is to hit, punch, bite, or fight. They are trying to release their anger and reset themselves. To help reduce aggression and fuel good and appropriate responses, we recommend helping children learn to find healthy coping skills to best process and manage those big negative emotions.

As you read through the early elementary stories, you will also notice that our students describe incidents only generally. This type of communication is part of their learning development. They are still learning to formulate stories and add specifics to create a visual of what is happening in their lives. Often, parents tell us that it is really difficult to get their children to talk about what happened at school. We recommend taking some strategies from the Stop and Think to develop a cheat sheet of questions to ask your child after school.

With the rise in technology, children are less socialized, and it is more difficult for them to interact with peers and express themselves. They resort to anger or often shut down. In this phase of their lives, they model a lot of norms, expectations, rules, or behaviors from their home environment. A child who comes from a more aggressive home might be more prone to push, shove, or yell at another child. A child of parents who are more absent might show attention-seeking behaviors or might seem aloof. In the last five years, we have seen a rise in selfish, mean behaviors and a decrease in empathy in young children. Many factors contribute to these new behaviors, such as less time with family in dual working households, over-packed schedules, more time in front of a tablet, and less time interacting and developing social skills.

Sadly, we have also found that more and more children don't even know their classmates' or peers' names. When they lose sight of people's names, those people are no longer persons to them and are more like entities or things that they find irrelevant. The first step in developing empathy is building connections. To build connections, children need to start learning each other's names and using them as much as they can. In elementary, you can easily use daily strategies to build connections to start to build empathy.

Each elementary student's story is unique, but within each story we found a powerful connection to the trends we see in elementary.

Definitions to Know
Bullying: Using your power over a period of time with the intention to harm someone else.

Drama: Back-and-forth conflict, gossip, rumors, or exclusion that create tension and fuel negative emotions.

Snitching/Tattling: Telling on someone to get them in trouble for doing something that is not harmful—for example, chewing gum in class, not listening to directions, talking during quiet time, being annoying, etc.

Telling: Telling on someone to save a life. Telling an adult that someone is in pain or being hurt.

Chapter 1: Learning Disability

Dear Bully,

I didn't and don't appreciate you bullying me, you make feel bad about myself like I am not important. It hurts me so much and I do not like feeling bad about myself, or always being angry and sad. You make me so angry. Please stop, please. I don't understand why you pick on me, what did I do to you?

The Victim

Dear Victim,

I'm annoyed at you. You keep talking, and you never pay attention in class. I'm always getting in trouble because I'm telling you to stop talking. I need silence to focus, and you distract me. By the time we hit recess, I'm so irritated, I just want to yell at you. You try to hang out with me, and I'm so angry with you. Give me some space. I just want you to go away.

I've never told anyone, but I have a learning disability. I know I'm quick with my words and my fists, but I struggle to read and write. I pretend to read during class, but all I see is a bunch of words. So when you distract me in class, I get upset. I don't want to bully you. I just want you to stop. I don't know how to ask for help. I'm embarrassed. Everyone knows how to read except me. I'm afraid I will repeat fourth grade.

Stop talking in class! I just need you to stop.

The Bully

Update: The Bully in this story dictated the letter to us, and we wrote it out for them. We had built trust over the course of our program, and they wanted to share how they felt about this peer.

Stop and Think

Classroom Management

This story between these two students is important because we have seen type of relationship this over and over in schools. A child can get irritated at another and bully the other in order to get them to stop being disruptive in class. More often than not, the bullying occurs with students struggling with learning disabilities. Some of the classrooms we work in have over thirty-five students and one teacher. Those numbers are a lot to manage for one professional.

Imagine that a child needs silence and focus, and a disruptive child keeps talking or moving. These distractions can escalate bullying behaviors. It is important to understand that bullying is more than a negative behavior; it is a result of feeling fear and pain. It can be fueled by past incidents, thoughts, and emotions.

One year, we noticed a larger amount of bullying being reported, and we found that it was due to other children being disruptive in class. The children who could not focus would target the disruptive children at recess, picking on the children, pushing them, excluding them, and yelling at them. Once we were able to gain more insight into the situation and help the teacher with classroom management, the bullying decreased. Digging deeper for the root cause of bullying can provide the best strategies to tackle an unclear bullying situation.

Chapter 2: In-Family Bullying

Dear Bully,

You cannot say bad things about me because I'm a girl. I don't understand why you have to be mean every time I see you... You manipulate our cousins to join in with you and I am left alone. I am always the outsider in our family. I hate that we all live in the same neighborhood and that I have to see you all the time. I hate going over to dinner at your place or when you and your mom come over. I just want to lock myself in my room. I hate you! My mom forces me to play with you.

Why do you only target me? Saying I suck at sports because I'm a girl, that I'm stupid because I am a girl, that I'm a psycho because I'm a girl is not right, its really hurtful and I need you to stop. Calling me ugly and fat over and over makes me furious. You push all of my buttons! You ruin every family function and I wish you would just not show up. Sometimes I wish you got sick so you didn't show up. You think you're being funny and everyone is laughing but I won't put up with it anymore. Just stop bullying me! I can't snitch but I am done. This has been going on forever. It is really rude and shows bad character.

Stop!

Your Cousin the Victim

Dear Victim,

I don't know what to say or even explain myself. I am sorry I bully you. It all started as a joke and now I can't seem to stop. I tease you because you get all the attention all the time. I guess I am a little jealous. It's so hard for me to admit. I'm embarrassed. I don't feel like I am good enough. I don't think I am good at anything. I am a loser.

When I am home, I hear my mom talk to your mom over the phone, and you are always the honor student, the athlete, the golden child. I heard my mom say she wished I acted more like you. She talks bad about me all the time. My mom never talks about me the way your mom talks about you. She puts me down every day. She reminds me that I am a mistake and that I'm annoying. She tells me I am lazy and I am a selfish brat. She never believes me when I tell her something happened to me. She always says I must have done something. Sometimes, I will be talking to her and it is important. She will be on her phone. She does not even listen to me anymore. She is always mad or stressed out. She says she does not have time for my bullshit.

I get picked on at school too. I get called stupid and kids make fun of me when I am at recess. When I see you, I am filled with rage, I can't compete with you. Our moms are always comparing us. It makes me sick.

Last week, I saw how I hurt your feelings, and I just could not help myself. I'm always getting in trouble since my dad left. He is too busy with his new family to even bother to call, my mom says. My life sucks. I can't tell you all this stuff, I am terrified you would laugh at me too. I know you might never forgive me and I don't know how to tell you that I am sorry. You never did anything to me. I wish I could turn back time and go back. Now I don't even know how to apologize.

I am sorry,

The Bully

Stop and Think

Forever Always Never (FAN) Syndrome
We mostly see the Forever Always Never syndrome in elementary school, and if not addressed, it follows the kids into middle school. We call it the FAN Syndrome. It is when a child uses blanket statements to talk about a person or a situation.

For example:
"I'm always excluded or left behind."
"This is always happening to me."
"She never stops teasing me."
"I never get what I want."

The FAN syndrome needs to be addressed so that kids understand that nothing is forever and that this moment too shall pass. We want to teach our kids that we live in a constantly changing environment and that nothing is permanent. If a child is being picked on, that does not mean that this will *always* happen. We want to eliminate the association of FAN with negative behaviors, so children can see that the behavior will cease and that it is not a forever thing. We work with children by explaining that often we use the FAN statement to protect ourselves from being hurt in the future.

The problem is that by using FAN, children set themselves up to be victimized or constantly targeted, because they adopt the attitude that the victimization or targeting will always happen, and they act in a way that almost attracts the unwanted behavior. A child who is excluded might start to think they will always be excluded. They isolate themselves and act distant or aloof with other kids. Over time, other kids are less likely to approach that child. We want to explore how situations might escalate to a FAN syndrome and address them. We do this work right in the moment. When running a girls' group, we encounter many friendship dramas and a ton of FAN syndrome. When the girls talk and we hear a FANning statement, we immediately stop the conversation and ask questions about the behavior.

For example:
Emma: "Lucie is always picking Anya and Ainslie over me and excluding me."
The Bully Teacher: "So you're saying that every day, every moment, and all the time, Lucie picks you last and excludes you?"
Emma: "*Yes*, always."
The Bully Teacher:" Well, if that's true, then why are you sitting next to Lucie?"
Emma: "Well, not this time, but every other time."
The Bully Teacher: "Aha! So not always, but more often than you like, she doesn't include you..."
Emma: "Yeah, I guess it's not always."
The Bully Teacher: "You see how that changes the way you see the situation? Your body language changed, your tone softened. By using 'always,' you make it a permanent thing, but every moment, you get a chance to make a different choice. Let's give Lucie the chance to make a different choice."

Chapter 3: Abusive Home

Dear Bully,

Please stop bullying it's not nice. Even though half the time I don't care. Stop hitting me. You make me cry. Stop being mean. Why do you always hit me at recess. I don't know what to do because I don't want to snitch on you because you'll just make fun of me more. I wish we could talk so you can understand you hurt me. I don't want to look weak or like a cry baby. I am not a scaredy cat, I want you to stop.

The Kid Being Hit

Dear Victim,

I am sorry I hit you. I wish I could stop. It is hard for me to talk about my anger. Bulldog is helping me, but it's hard for me. My anger takes over. I sometimes get so mad I think about kicking or throwing stuff. I am angry all the time. When I get in trouble for hitting you, I go home and my dad beats me.

I know you don't know this but, I get a whopping at home for speaking up, for acting up, or for being in the same room as my pops. I am not good with my words, so when you make me mad, all I know what to do is hit.

He calls me a sissy, fag, a loser, laughs at me, tells me I am going to end up like my older brother. My brother died from a drive-by last year. Him and his friends laugh at me while they sit in the living room and drinking beer. He tells me if my mom wasn't such a crack whore, he would send me back to her. I sit in my room and I am filled with rage. I can hear him going to the fridge getting another beer and walking back to the couch at night. I am terrified when he is drunk, it gets really bad. I think about how much I want to hurt him. Then I get so angry at you.

Why do you snitch? I sit and think about how you got me in trouble and that I want to hit you even more. I am stuck in this crappy house. I don't know what to do anymore, I am close to being suspended. I don't know what will happen if I am home for three days. I am terrified of my pops. I need help.

The Bully

Update: The story above was reported by our team. The house was evaluated, and the child was removed from the home. He was placed with his grandmother. After the child was removed from the home, there was a significant positive change in his behavior and attitude. We will never know the severity of his abuse, but with the help of his grandma, counselor, and the school, he got the support he needed.

Stop and Think

Discipline or Abuse
There is a fine line between discipline and abuse. In this case, we got involved because of the severity of the parent's behavior and its impact on the child, but at other times, the family's behavior is hard for us to define.

In this particular case, we found that this boy, in his urban setting, was more prone to lie and be aggressive if blamed for bullying than his peers would be. This child had what we could best describe as "emotional tantrums." He screamed, yelled, tried to hit the other children, and often ended up crying because of the outburst. When the tears came, it was a moment of emotional release in which to try to connect with him. We found that the emotional tantrums and lying were due to being over-disciplined and abused at home. He did not want to get beaten at home, so he lied about what he had done at school. Lying was a means of survival for him. He felt trapped in a vicious cycle that we are still trying to understand and navigate.

This particular case illustrates a difficult and uncomfortable topic for us to write about and discuss, but we feel it should be addressed. Remember that disciplining occurs in every house, in some shape or form. We should stay mindful of our stances on physical punishment. Before we jump to conclusions, we must be aware that most physical punishment leads to emotional trauma or physical harm.

Chapter 4: Snitching Culture

Dear Bully,

Why do you hurt me? Why do you pick on me everyday and make me not want to come to school. I hate school, I can't focus and I am afraid to snitch. Please stop or go away!

Afraid to snitch

Dear Afraid to Snitch,

I am truly sorry that you get picked on every day. The pain that can cause can really impact how you feel about yourself. I want you to see your story from our perspective. Remember how it feels when you get picked on by the bully. Identify your emotions. Think about what makes you hate school the most, then identify the rooms at school that you might be afraid to enter because of the bully. Now, imagine your little sister, brother, cousin, or best friend. Think about why you love them and how much they mean to you.

Imagine that they are being bullied just like you. They feel what you feel when a bully attacks them.

Wouldn't you want to tell a teacher, tell the counselor, or tell your parents? Do you want someone else to feel the way you feel?

I believe that you would want to help and protect the people you love. Do the same for yourself. Be brave, just like a superhero. Superheroes protect the people whom they love; they protect the innocent; they help people; they speak on behalf of someone they care about. Think about who your favorite superhero is. Imagine you have their power to save people. Take that courage, and talk to your parents, teachers, counselor, or principal. Be that superhero. Superheroes help and protect, so be the superhero that I know you are.

I also want to let you in on something that might activate your superhero powers. Often, if a bully is picking on you, there is probably another student going through the same bullying as you. They might need a superhero. You never know. Maybe the other student is fed up and really sad. By speaking up, you give them a chance to love school and to be happy.

You're saving his life!

I'm not kidding you. One day a superhero told me this: "Tattling or snitching is getting someone in trouble on purpose, *but* telling is saving someone's life."

Don't hold back your superpowers, but speak up when you know you could be really helping someone in pain.

Don't forget. When a person bullies anyone, they're in pain; they are suffering. They need help and often don't even know how to ask for it. You would be a superhero for the bully, too. You would stop a cycle, and you would start to see a difference in your school. We see it all the time. All I need you to do is to believe in yourself and be the amazing superhero who is going to end bullying in your school.

Sending you strength and power with lots of love and positivity, my incredible Superhero,

The Bully Teacher

Update: In this letter, there was a lot of repetition of the word "superhero." Our goal was to be consistent in the message, so the child saw the value of standing up for themselves. By using "superhero" versus "advocate," we were able to make the situation more relatable.

Stop and Think

Tattling Disease

Our society has a really big problem with the words "snitch" and "tattling," part of an old-school mentality that trickles down into our younger generation and has a severe negative impact on children who ask for help. As parents and educators, we need to change the narrative.

In our programs, we teach that tattling means getting someone in trouble on purpose; telling is saving someone's life. When a child tells, they are trying to stop the pain or the negative behavior. They are not trying to get someone in trouble. We need to clarify these definitions with our children and be clear about the importance of telling an adult when they are in danger, in pain, or suffering. We emphasize the telling by sharing that if a child is being bullied, they are most probably not the only one, and by telling they might even save another child's life. We don't want to underestimate a child's pain or emotional state.

We need to start opening up and telling people when we are hurt. When kids repress their pain and keep from telling, they create a large amount of stress for themselves. This repression impacts their self-esteem and self-worth. We want kids, especially at a young age, to tell us when they are being hurt or are in pain. We can help them and give them the tools to overcome the negative behaviors they experience.

Examples of Telling:
"Mom, I'm being pushed into the lockers every day and I get pinned in the bathroom by this group of kids. I don't know what to do. I'm afraid to use the bathroom."

"Teacher, the girls at recess pick on me. They laugh at my clothes and make fun of me. They call me dirty and go around the playground, telling everyone I smell."

Examples of Tattling:

"Mom, Bobby isn't doing his homework."
"Dad, Addy is *not* going to bed now."
"Teacher, Mason is chewing gum."
"Principal, Olivia is late again and didn't pick up her tardy note."

Chapter 5: Apologies Wanted and No Room for Forgiveness

Dear Bully,

I would greatly appreciate it if you would stop making fun of me. You make me sad. If you say sorry I would be willing to accept your apology! Can you apologize? I don't understand why it's so hard to say sorry or to stop picking on me.

Apology Wanted

Dear Victim,

I am sorry I make you sad. I make fun of you because you bullied me in second grade. You made fun of my clothes, called me dirty, and made fun of how I could not read. I am angry and I can't forgive you. You pretend like you never did that and call me a liar. I can't forgive you. You never apologized to me. I miss you as my friend, but I won't be the one to say sorry first. I am not weak.

The Bully

Stop and Think

Resentment and Learning to Let Go
The letters above are examples of desired apologies, trying to let go, old grudges, and resentment. We often read these types of letters in our programs. Apologies and letting go can be difficult for all of us, even as adults. We need to help children learn the skill of forgiveness and letting go, to help them as they get older.

Children can often hold onto something that is painful, and they replay it in their minds. They do not want to let it go. It becomes part of their story. In our programs, we work on rewriting their story in order to move forward. Forgiveness is so hard, but children get stronger each time they let go, forgive, and move on.

Someone who holds grudges and resentment is often unforgiving and typically comes across as judgmental and snarky. They are negative, and they make hurtful comments. They never seem strong or courageous. We must learn from them and teach our kids to apologize and let go. We want them to learn resilience, strength, and grit. By letting go and forgiving people, they gain those skills. A child who forgives and lets go knows that they can start over and have a second chance. They grow up more emotionally grounded and prepared for challenges. When a child holds onto grudges and resentment, they accumulate pain and miss opportunities for joy and love. Over the years, the pain accumulates and gets heavy. The child carries these grudges, resentments, and anger, with no room to let other people in. These burdens make for an emotionally underdeveloped child.

Because many children still see forgiveness as weak, we have had to get creative in our teaching of this subject. We have asked students to help each other create strategies to let go and forgive. Some of the questions we have asked during the post-activity discussion groups are:
 "Why is it hard to forgive people?"
"Why is forgiveness seen as weak?" "What makes forgiving people and moving on weak?"
"Why is it important to forgive someone you love?"
"When you make a mistake, why do you want someone to forgive you?"
"How does it feel when you hold grudges or resentment towards a person?"
"If you got into a fight with a friend, why would you want them to forgive you?"
"When someone says, 'I forgive you,' how does it feel?"
"Share a time you let go and forgave someone. How did it feel?"
"When you keep thinking about someone who hurts you, what feelings come up?"
"How do you act around people who you don't want to forgive?"
"What does it feel like when someone forgives you for something you have done?"
"How have you moved forward when someone has hurt you and has said, 'I'm sorry'?"

In asking similar questions, you can build a connection between forgiveness and the importance of letting go. This process is about identifying negative emotions and talking through them to help overcome pain. Then, you focus on how to mend, rebuild, or start over with more positive emotions. We encourage you to use this time to talk to your children and help them understand the importance of forgiveness and apologies. You can share a story about a time you forgave someone who hurt you.

Story Sample to Adapt to Your Own Parenting Style:

Mom: "A few years ago, your dad forgot my birthday. He didn't get me a present, or a card, or send me a text to wish me happy birthday. I was sad, angry, lonely, frustrated, confused, ashamed. I felt I was not good enough to be celebrated. I went the entire day being mad at him. He came home from work, and I just lost my temper. He was really apologetic. He had honestly made a mistake. He had looked at the calendar and thought that my birthday was the next day. Since I hadn't talked about it and hadn't shared with him what I wanted, he didn't really notice the days flying by. He said he was really sorry. In that moment, I had a choice. I could
   a) Be snarky and mean to him all night and go to bed hurt. (not letting go)
   b) Constantly bring up the fact that he forgot about my birthday and make him feel bad. (resentment)
   c) Accept his apology and understand that he did make an honest mistake. (forgiveness)

So I took a deep breath and said, "I forgive you" as I exhaled. It felt really good. I felt a release, like I could start over. That night, we cooked dinner as a family, and we had so much fun. Dad was being so goofy and caring. We rented movies and cuddled. He even snuck a candle into the carton of ice cream, and you both sang me Happy Birthday. Do you remember that, Ben?
Ben: "Yeah, Mom. You said it was the best birthday! Were you lying?"
Mom: No, Ben, it actually was an amazing birthday. Because I forgave Dad and let go of my hurt, I was able to let love into our evening. Everything shifted. It was amazing. That's the power of forgiveness.

Chapter 6: Sibling Bullying Cycle

Dear Big Sister,

I know I have called you fat and ugly and I realized it is super wrong. I did it because I was mad at you. We fight so much, and I know you are self-conscious about your weight. I know that calling you fat will get you pissed off and you will stop ignoring me or making fun of me. I don't think you are fat, I don't think you are ugly. You are beautiful and I love being around you. I wish you would include me more, I wish you would say hi in the hallways at school and pay attention to me. I look up to you and when you ignore me I get so mad, I want to scream at you.

Love,

Little Sister

Dear Little Sister,

I feel bad, I get caught up in our fights and drama, I get enraged with you. I didn't see that you really needed me, until the other day. It hurts when you call me fat, ugly, and yelled at me. I want to slam the door on your face. I want to hurt you so bad because I am hurting. Even if you are younger, your words hurt me. I am really self-conscious of my weight and looks.

It irritates me, Mom is constantly comparing herself to me. It's weird. Why does she do that? I keep hearing her stories of how she was an extra small when she was my age. She reminds me I would never fit in her clothes. It is really embarrassing when she tells my friends about how popular she was in high school. I am dreading going to high school.

I am ashamed of who I am, I will never be like Mom. You are so much like Mom, I get jealous I guess. You and her are thin, and I am fat. I feel gross and when you call me names, it makes it more real. I feel like I don't fit into this family. I feel like I will never live up to Mom's expectations. I am sorry for ignoring you at school, for screaming at you to get out of my room. I thought you were doing it to annoy me.

Now going through this program, I see you might actually be reaching out to me. I will work on being nicer and including you. I don't want you to feel the way I do about myself. I am sorry for pushing you away.

Love,

Big Sister

Stop and Think

The Impact of Comparing and Contrasting
These letters illustrate a common phenomenon we wish no daughters ever had to experience. We also wish we didn't have to write about it, because we don't like to tell parents how to parent. We went back and forth about how to present this issue, because we see it more than we would like to admit. More and more, in our programs, we hear (mostly) girls say that their moms talk about their pasts and compare their childhood to that of their children. We want to have a heart-to-heart with mothers. As women, we are so used to being judged, criticized, and put down, we might not even realize we are doing it to our daughters. Offhand comments like these can often be worst for girls.

For the sake of this story, we focus on young teenage girls and their relationships to their mothers. We need to have these uncomfortable conversations to make progress in building our daughters' self-esteem.

When moms compare themselves to their daughters, they can have a painful and detrimental effect on their daughters' self-esteem. As mothers, as women, we have the power to truly impact our daughters.

As our children grow up, it can be hard not to impose our own yucky stuff on them. We might be triggered by their experiences or the phase that they might be encountering. We might remember our own experiences and have some negative emotions. We might not want our children to suffer the way we have, or we might want to guide them to better choices through our own experiences. The problem is that we have not overcome our own experiences, and we not have quite processed our own pain, and more often than not, we project our own feelings onto our daughters.

It is time for us, as women and mothers, to let go of our pasts and stop projecting them onto our children. We want to create more self-awareness about the effect of our words. When a mother talks about her past middle or high school experiences and either compares them to her daughter's experiences or brags about them, this mother can create an internal conflict for her daughter and the way she feels about her own experiences, in comparison to those of her mother.

In this story, the child clearly feels a comparison to her mother and criticism about not being a certain weight. She also feels ostracized because of her size and by her own perceived lack of accomplishment, as she does not fit the mold she thinks her mom desires.

The following are some toxic statements that girls have shared with us in our group sessions:

"I was so cool in high school. I would never have been seen in band."
"I was Prom Queen, and I didn't even try to get it."

"When I was your age, I had to work hard to be fit."
"You should eat that."
"Don't you think you've had enough...?"
"I would have never done that."
"I can't believe you said or did that to your friend. I would never have done that."
"You are too sensitive. Get over it."
"Stop being so dramatic!"
"You're always causing so much drama."
"You don't even know what it is to struggle…"
"I was so pretty when I was your age…"
"Middle school was so easy for me…"
"I loved high school. I was so popular."
"My clothes would never fit you."
"I had so many friends in middle and high school."
"You look fat in that outfit."
"What did you do to your hair?"
"You have too much makeup. You look like a whore or a clown."

The following are some positive statements that mothers could use instead:
"You look so beautiful."
"You don't need any makeup. You are naturally beautiful."
"I was super awkward in middle school, and I love how I turned out."
"You don't have to get sucked into the drama. Be your own person."
"You are stunning."
"I wish I looked like you at your age."
"You look so much like me. I'm so lucky to see your beauty shine."
"I went through the same phase, and I wish my mom said this to me…"
"I love your creativity with your makeup. I also love when you just go natural."
"I like that outfit, but it does not really express who you are."

We get a little frustrated by moms who correct us in elementary school and tell us not to focus on their children's looks. Although mothers may think that they do not want to dwell on their daughters' beauty, their daughters are beautiful, and we hope that mothers will boost their daughters' self-esteem with positive statements like the ones above. We have never met a girl in elementary or middle school who felt that her mom told her she was too beautiful.

Parents should focus on their daughters' skills and academics, but we hope they will not forget that beauty counts. Daughters are already focused on how they look to others. They look at themselves in the mirror and in their phones, and they need to see their beauty and understand what makes them unique, glorious, and beautiful. We want to flaunt their beauty. We do not ask mothers to demean their daughters by focusing only on their bodies, but we believe that beauty can go hand and hand with intelligence. It is not an "either/or." If mothers do not share how much they love every aspect of their daughters, middle school, for those daughters, will be a battle for self-esteem. Those same mothers worry about their outfits, their hair, the weight they have gained, how their makeup looks; their daughters worry about these same issues. By not sharing when they look good, mothers silence their daughters' personalities and identities. Mothers should say, "You are beautiful and smart. I love your body and your powerful brain. I love your outfit and how you rocked math." These positive statements can create "and" situations that will build girls up to love their bodies and not dismiss them." Mothers can help them love their bodies, as their bodies are conduits to their souls.

Chapter 7: Roasting and Teasing

Dear Bully,

I don't understand why you are so rude to me! I don't understand why you call me names. I've seen you do this to other girls and some boys, too. It really hurts my feelings. That's not ok. I really need you to stop. You've been doing this since I was in 1st grade. Stop it!

Annoyed

Dear Annoyed,

I am sorry for what I did. I didn't know I was hurting anyone until I saw you talk to Bulldog. Everyone laughs at my jokes, so I keep coming up with more jokes to be funny. No one told me that I was hurting people, I didn't know. I feel bad, I thought people were laughing at my jokes, now I can see that people are laughing because they are afraid of me. I saw your face yesterday, I am aware of how my teasing is hurting everyone.

Please accept my apology,

The Bully

Stop and Think

Roasting and Teasing

The story above illustrates the fact that many children do not know the difference between teasing and bullying.

Bullying is using your power to intentionally hurt someone over a period of time.

Teasing is a lot more complicated. Even as adults, we have trouble with the boundaries of teasing. There are three types of teasing: good teasing, unintentional mean teasing, and bad teasing.

Good teasing is when a friend makes fun of someone in order to connect, to make that person laugh, to have that person like them more.

For example:
Imitating a friend to make them laugh.
Repeating something a friend said to laugh and show you care.
Picking on a friend to ease the situation.
Making jokes about a situation to make a friend feel at ease.

Bad teasing is when someone purposely targets someone else in order to make fun of them. Often, this is done by roasting or by teasing someone over time without understanding the impact of the teasing words.

For example:
Repeating something your friend said in a condescending way.
Being overly sarcastic to make a point.
Targeting a friend and teasing them about who they like, how they dress, or who they identify with.
Teasing a friend about a challenge or failure.
Repeating a secret and making it funny or embarrassing.

Unintentional mean teasing is the one to watch for. It is a type of teasing between building connection and mean roasting. Unintentional mean teasing is when a friend takes a joke too far. In Dear Bully Assemblies, kids often talk about roasting and how it hurts. They have done it, and they almost feel it is a rite of passage in friendship. At Bulldog, we scratch our heads and wonder when it became ok to roast other people.

Friends know each other's darkest secrets, their insecurities, the people they like, and the drama in their homes. So when they roast one other, they use the "good stuff," intimate information that is painful and embarrassing. In these situations, friends actually have more power than a random bully. They know how to harm when they roast. How does one handle the dynamic of roasting? What can we do to react to it? Let's play this out as adults...

Imagine someone is with their best friend from college or high school, and that best friend suddenly makes fun of the person's marriage, makes jokes about their child, and jabs them about their anxiety. The best friend puts them down about their work and tells embarrassing stories. Would the person really hang out with that friend again? As an adult, would someone put up with a friend who is so mean and inconsiderate? We don't think so. We hope not.

But children put up with these relationships in order to be cool. Kids pretend roasting of this type is ok, but in our one-on-one sessions, they talk about how their friends bully them, all because of the roasting epidemic.

At its worst, mean teasing often leads to bullying—not always, but if the teasing is not addressed, it can turn very quickly. When a child feels attacked, they go dark. In middle school, we have seen kids call each other "dirty," "nasty," "skanky," "ugly," "fat," "whore," "stupid," "dump," "retarded," "loser," "piece of shit," "scaredy-cat," "pussy," and the list goes on. These words are painful and can be hurtful to hear.

These words come from our child's environment—the shows they watch, the kids they hang around with, the language they hear at home. A second grader calling another girl a slut or a whore has no idea of the impact of the words; she just knows how they hurt. She might have seen her mom cry over the terms, when her dad used them. A boy laughing at his friend on the basketball court, calling him a wimp or pussy, is exhibiting a learned behavior.

We see this type of mean teasing in our groups of friends, and then we see it transmitted to our children. Jabs happen all the time; we must call them out and apologize to one another. We need to put our foot down and share why it is not okay to roast friends. We should talk about how our friends treat us and about the power of trust. We need to be open about how it is not okay for a friend to share secrets as a joke. We need to start creating a line in the sand about appropriate and inappropriate teasing.

Strategies to Address Teasing:

If a child is experiencing teasing, we should try to examine the teasing from the child's point of view by finding a time to sit down with the child and talk about what is happening. We can have the child describe what is going on by saying, "Tell me what is happening." We can ask, " Who is teasing you?"; " How does that make you feel?"; " Why do you think the person is teasing you?" We must not forget to validate the child's feelings when they express how they feel and what is happening.

We must remember not to overreact and to encourage the child to make friends with and hang out with others who make them feel good about themselves. We must remember also to look at ourselves. Have we teased others or lost our cool? We can talk about these actions and how we felt. These are great moments to connect and learn from each other. Children will easily pick up on and mirror a grownup's actions. The more we are aware, the better our kids can take action.

Chapter 8: Racial Bullying, Stereotypes, and Language Barriers

Language Barriers

Dear Bulldog,

I used to be teased by people saying that I was dumb because from Kindergarten to 2nd grade I didn't know how to speak English or even read it. It got to the point that it hurt me so much that I stopped going to school, so I wouldn't be bullied. When my mom used to make me go, I used to cry because I didn't want to go to school because I knew the bullying would continue. I wish they were nicer to me. I faked being sick all the time. It has stopped now the bullying, but I still can't get over how much that hurt me.

Language Barrier

Dear Language Barrier,

I am so sorry to hear that you were bullied due to a language barrier. I can imagine how you feel about being teased. This is out of your control. In early elementary, it's so important to feel safe and supported. I can relate to your story. I went through the same thing...

I'm French Canadian. My entire elementary school, I struggled with learning to read and write. I didn't speak the language. Teachers called me slow and dumb. I was pulled from class all the time, and I had an IEP. I was so embarrassed to be constantly pulled out of class. I just wanted to be normal.

What I didn't know at the time, but I do now is that speaking a second language is a superpower. It opens so many doors and gives us an opportunity for different jobs across the world. It's a hidden superpower that will take you a long way. Embrace it and work really hard to learn all aspects of English. Once you do, learning a third language is a breeze.

Learning languages opens different parts of your brain, and it gives you the ability to better understand all that surrounds you. When I was growing up, I never walked into a room not understanding what was being said. I could understand both languages. I was able to translate for my mom and dad and speak on their behalf. It might not have been ideal at the time, but it helped me be a better advocate, gain more ability to translate on the spot, and lead conversations to avoid any miscommunications.

Speaking another language is a gift, and when we use it, the most powerful stuff can happen. You can stop a fight, a miscommunication. You can help someone in need; you can translate for others; you can tutor; you can be a teacher's helper at Parent Teacher Conferences. You can write and read all you want in whichever language. That is powerful. This reminds me of the quote by Frank Smith: "One language sets you in a corridor for life. Two languages open every door along the way."

I am sorry that you were bullied and had to go through this, but I hope you now know what a great superpower you have. Maybe you can use this experience to help others who are experiencing the same thing you have. Maybe if you see someone struggling with a language, you can help them, or just be kind to that person and make them feel welcome. What are some things you can do to make someone feel included if they are different?

Be the advocate you want others to be for you. It will bring you great joy.

Je t'envoie beaucoup de courage et de l'amour.

The Bully Teacher

Racial Bullying and Stereotypes

Dear Bully,

You bullied me because I was Asian and because I had a bowl cut. You called me "China Boy" but I am Filipino, so it really annoyed me. You make funny faces when I walk by and make fun of me. Every time we get our test back you grab my paper and say, of course you got an A China Boy. You push me around and mock me in front of our peers. You tell people that your mom and friends go to my parents nail salon. You make up these stories about me, and they are not even true. My parents work really hard. They left their country to give me a better life. I can't tell them what you are doing to me. They would not understand. They would be disappointed. They can't really speak English, so I would have to translate to my teacher or principal what is going on. That is more embarrassing than you bullying me. I can forgive you but please stop. I just want to get good grades to make my parents proud. I am tired of being attacked for being smart. I work really hard.

The Victim

Dear Victim,

It's hurtful to be bullied for things such as our hair, because it is something that we wear with pride and shows us to the world. It is a whole different feeling to be bullied for something we absolutely cannot control—our race. To take it a step further, to misidentify race can also be hurtful. I have experienced it. I know how it can be painful. I am biracial—half black, half white. I spent my entire life in between a racial divide, trying to find my place.

It is funny to think about, but when you look at me, most people will identify me as black but not white. It is like I am "either/or." I can't be the two of them. It can hurt when someone doesn't recognize your identity. It hurts me, because with our identity come stereotypes and biases.

And in your case, the bully defaults to Chinese because they do not know any better. They don't understand you, and they are targeting you. It is really frustrating, and it can also be confusing.

It sounds like you feel comfortable forgiving this person if they stop picking on you. That is a great first step. I would find a teacher or staff member that you trust. It could be your homeroom teacher, your art teacher, your gym teacher, or even the amazing lady at the front desk. Find someone that you trust and explain what is going on. Tell them how it makes you feel and how it impacts your focus. Tell them how you value education and you don't want this impacting your grades. Then share with them how you want to solve this problem. You can do a mediation to talk through everything. I am guessing that this bully is hurt, and they are using their words as weapons. Maybe if you talk more, you can find out why they are in so much pain. It could be a lot of reasons, but often when you get targeted for being smart, the other child is suffering. So here are some more solutions:
- Have a "Dirt Digging" Session. This is when you dig up all the old dirt between the two of you to find out where everything fell apart.
- Have the teacher change the seating arrangement so you can sit together and work on projects.
- Get paired up for a project so both of you can bring your strengths to the table.
- Have them help you with something that might be more difficult.
- Work together on homework or go to peer tutoring.
- Have a weekly or monthly lunch check-in with them and a counselor, to talk about the progress of your relationship.
- Do an Around the World project with your class. Each week, peers share about their heritage and upbringing.

Stay proud of where you came from. Everyone is unique. It is differences like these that keep life interesting.

Sending you Love and Positivity,

The Bully Teacher

Stop and Think

Racial Bullying, Stereotypes, and Language Barriers

Diversity brings different ideas and outcomes into the classroom. It can be magical and create innovative ideas, thought-provoking conversations, and new outcomes to difficult problems. Diversity can also be difficult to address. In our line of work, we talk about race, biases, and stereotypes all the time. They are still difficult issues to address. Words have power and carry a lot of weight. Some words carry burden, resentment, and pain. Other words bring up painful, traumatic memories. We need to have more and more conversations about race earlier in elementary school. We need to set expectations early, so later in life, we don't use words as weapons. Early on, children are curious and want to learn. They often don't quite see color as we do. They see different tones of skin, but all they see is the skin, not what it represents. We want to instill in these beautiful developing minds more openness and awareness. Having conversations about race in class and sharing different experiences can be extremely powerful. Introducing "Culture Days" and inviting the parents can create new connections.

Sadly, children's racial views come from home. Home life influences many children's approaches to diversity and to celebrating others' differences.

As adults, we sometimes forget how many of our words are absorbed by the children in our lives. Two years ago, we were working in a school where some of the students were excluding and bullying some of the Latino students, not all of whom were Mexican. When we finally spoke to the Latino students and they felt they could open up to us, they told us that other students said that "They should go back to their own country" and that they were going to "create a wall around the school to kick all you Mexicans out." One child said that these "Mexicans are stealing all of our jobs and committing crimes in our city." Re-read that sentence one more time. These are the words of a third grader. I don't know too many elementary students who worry about the job market or crime rate. Our children use our lenses to better see the world. If our lenses are skewed or tainted with fear or hate, then we impose those views on our own children.

Experiences among children like these break my heart, not only because certain kids get bullied, but also because when the other children are older, they perpetuate a cycle of hate. This pattern can be changed by monitoring what we say around children, by not being too harsh, and by educating ourselves with facts and being open to new ideas. Oppression, hate crimes, discrimination, bullying, harassment, and violence happen every day. It is sad, painful, and unnecessary. We live in a world of abundance, in a country of unlimited resources, and in a global community that is constantly connected. When we express feelings of fear or lack, then we can push our hateful beliefs on our children. Our homes and classrooms are the best places to start the fight against racial bullying.

To elaborate on our point, we share another example. Almost three years ago, we worked at a school that was about 85% white and 15% Latino. We were talking about stereotypes and how to address them. We did a role-play commercial activity. One student raised his hand and said, "I love my friend Alessandra. I don't believe that her parents are stealing our jobs. I don't believe that she's dirty, and I don't think she's dumb because she speaks Spanish. But what do I do when my parents say this stuff at the dinner table?"

We were put in the very uncomfortable position of speaking from the heart and being safe, even if that meant possibly criticizing Ben's parents. We said, "Ben, I don't know your mom or dad, but I'm sure they're great people. I'm sure you love them very much and don't want to disappoint them. We get that and want to show you a different side of this story. We want you to know that sometimes our parents' views are wrong or one-sided. When it comes to discipline, grades, and safety, *always* listen to your parents, but when it comes to hate and racism, Ben, make up your own mind. You have the power to re-educate your parents, to speak up for your friend, and make a small difference in your home."

Ben's question opened up, in our session, such a powerful discussion about how to re-educate our parents and grandparents about race. A child just needs to speak up in order to create awareness. Over time, the awareness takes hold, fear start to subside, and our hearts open up to new perspectives and ideas. Fear is the most dangerous emotion. It drives hateful thoughts and sometimes irreparable actions. Fear closes us off to the world and keeps us small. Listening to some of the things our children are learning in school can often be really beneficial to us.

Children are sponges, and they often take our words literally. Much work is done in schools to make the world more accepting and inclusive. Companies spend millions on diversity training, implicit bias programs, and inclusive initiatives. But this work is only effective if it is continued at home. How can we, as educators and parents, open the doors to building more inclusive homes? What can we do in our homes to continue these conversations?

Ideas to increase diversity in your classroom:
- Hang up a map and have students pin where their family comes from. Each week, pick a new location and have students create a report that includes geography, history, sociology, cultural facts, and much more.
- Have Culture Family Days, where parents and children share food and traditions from their homes.
- Bring more culturally diverse books into your classroom. Add new fables or stories that introduce culturally diverse perspectives.
- Connect with classrooms around the world and have a pen pal project.
- Do a community project to learn the different cultures within the school community.
- Celebrate diverse holidays or discuss different religious celebrations and learn about their meanings and histories.
- Introduce song, dance, art, and music to learn more about different cultures.
- Do interview activities that build conversations about traditions in different homes.

Ideas to increase diversity in your home:
- Invite parents over from your child's class and get to know them.
- Cook or order out ethnic food and have a conversation about traditions and backgrounds around the culinary experience.

- Attend different cultural events to learn about your diverse community.
- Watch different ethnic movies or shows with your family.
- Add culturally diverse books to your library.
- Read diverse books to your child.
- When you hear or see something racially charged, say something and have a conversation with your child.
- Have theme night dance parties with your family.
- For family vacation, have your family create a report or PowerPoint about their preferred destination and the culture of that vacation spot.
- Diversify your friend group.
- Diversify your play groups.
- Introduce new vegetables, fruits, and plants to your family, and learn about them.
- Explore your city and its cultural experiences.

Behaviors like the ones from the bully in the letter don't often happen in front of adults, because children usually associate some guilt with saying things like this, or they are fearful of being punished at school, but they may know that this kind of speech is acceptable at home. This difference is confusing to the child and creates contrast. It is up to us to break the cycle by pushing ourselves out of our comfort zones and learning with our children. One simple step can start a movement or a revolution and can create a monumental change. I think we can all agree that one little step is easy for us to take, to see the ripple effect it will have on our children.

Chapter 9: Cyberbullying/Online Safety

Dear Victim,

Sorry for bullying you online. I made fun of you because you didn't know how to play. I hope you can forgive me, you're actually pretty cool. I just got into the game and I was excited and I wanted to look cool in front of my other online friends. When I saw that attacking you online got everyone going, I didn't know how to stop. I am sorry that each time you got back into the game, I would attack you and write you mean messages on your board. I just got so obsessed with winning. It was like the only thing that mattered to me. I think about this game all the time. My parents tell me I am addicted, so at night when they sleep I jump online and play. I made some new friends and those are the ones I am trying to impress. I really like Sexy Kitty, she seems cool. She says she goes to the other neighborhood school. She's so good at the game and is showing me all these tricks. When she saw you were beating me at the game, she told me to make fun of you. She even told me what to say. I don't even know what some of the stuff meant. I just did it so she would still be my friend. I hope I can meet her someday.

Real Sorry

Dear Real Sorry,

We need to have yet another heart-to-heart. I guarantee that Sexy Kitty is not in elementary school. I would be surprised if this kitty cat is even in school. She is pressuring you to say mean things to your friend, and you don't even know what some of the stuff means. That can get you into some major trouble.

This is super important. Do not give your address or send your picture to Sexy Kitty. We want you to talk to your parents, because, Real Sorry, this is dangerous! When we play online games, we meet people from all over and of all ages. Sexy Kitty is a great example. People online sometimes lie and make us do things that might be dangerous or hurtful. You don't want to associate with these people *ever*. We recommend that you apologize in person to your friend and tell them the whole story.

We are also getting involved and working with your parents to help you stay safe online.

Sending Positivity and strength,

The Bully Teacher

Stop and Think

Cyberbullying / Online Safety

We have run into cyberbullying quite a bit while delivering programs across the country. In elementary school, cyberbullying is less frequent, but the above situation happens more than we ever thought possible. It is time to talk about online safety.

Here are some simple strategies to keep elementary school children safe online:

1. Restrict online use to a common area of the home. This is an easy way to monitor what your child is doing and to pay attention to their online friends and conversations.
2. Get familiar with the games or apps the kids are using. Talk to your child about which ones they use, and talk regularly with them about their online usage, about what is happening in chats, and about gaming strategies. Listen attentively and try to pay attention to your child's cues. Do they have a team mentality? Do they find joy in the game? Do they want to win at all costs? Do they fear that if they don't play, they might be excluded? By figuring out your child's intentions, you can build conversations about their online behaviors and friends.
3. Pay attention to the amount of time your child spends online. If you think your kid is watching too much YouTube or is online too much, my gut tells me you are right. Find alternative activities and give your children examples of what they can do besides being online. Being bored is a good thing. Children can let their imaginations run wild for a little bit. Limit screen time to one to two hours a day if you can.
4. Have a reward or some sort of incentive, for the days your child stays off gaming devices.
5. Have daily chats about their online friends or shows. By doing this, you build open communication and trust between yourself and your child. Ask open-ended questions and be curious.
6. Let your child help set boundaries or rules for gaming and tablet use. You will have more buy-in, and they will feel more empowered.
7. Use Common Sense to review apps or shows: https://www.commonsense.org
8. Be vigilant about not sleeping with tablets or not using tablets too close to bedtime.
9. Keep doors open and pop into the room to check on the game when children are gaming. You can even use Alexa or Google to drop in to do a quick drive-by.
10. Explain your *why*. Be clear about why online safety is important and why you are monitoring their games and friends. Talk about the dangers of oversharing information and about creepers online. We want our kids to be aware of the possible dangers so they can think about their actions and make better choices. By setting expectations, rules, and boundaries you create a clear path to online safety.

Remember that we want to keep an open line of communication with our child, all the while trying to keep them as safe as possible from the drama and bullying that can occur online during this age. Vigilance can be a full-time job, and we must have these conversations early. If a child has an iPad, it is already time to chat about online safety.

Chapter 10: The Power of Positive Affirmations

Dear Bulldog,

I have been bullied when I was in younger grades where they would call me names and be rude then get mad at me. It really hurt me and makes me feel that something was wrong with me. I am sad I feel like I will never be enough.

Not Enough

Dear Not Enough,

I am sorry that you were bullied in early elementary and that they would call you names and be rude to you. It sounds like you were in a lot of pain. When I read your letter, I feel like you are still holding onto that pain and making it a part of you. There is nothing wrong with you. I would feel hurt, too, with the anger, rudeness, and name-calling; that is a lot to deal with at a young age.

I would like you to let go of your pain.

Think of a way to feel better. I know that as you read this, you might think that letting go is impossible, but I know you can do it. You know, the kids who teased you were hurt, too. A bully is never a cool kid, loving life, and happy-go-lucky. It is a person in pain. What they did and said to you is not ok, but there is a way for you to start feeling better.

Carrying all your pain is like carrying a heavy backpack filled with rocks. It hurts, and it is so heavy to carry. Visualize a backpack that you are carrying, and start thinking of each name or incident as a rock. Imagine how heavy the backpack feels to carry, how hard it is for you to stand up straight. Think about the weight on your shoulders. It makes you tired. It makes you react slower. It holds you down.

Now, slowly imagine taking a rock out of the backpack. Think about how it would feel to be a little lighter, a little more free. Think about each rock you carry and what it represents to you. Then, name the rock you pulled out of the backpack, and let it fall to the ground. Take a deep breath in as you visualize yourself pulling each rock out of the backpack and remember its name, and take a deep breath out to release the rock and drop it to the ground.

Say to yourself, "I am not defined by these rocks. I am not defined by these names."

Do this until you empty your backpack. Now, refill the backpack with joy and strength.

Make a list of all the stuff that you like about yourself or that you used to like about yourself. Write down all the stuff that makes you unique or brings you joy. Use "I am" statements.

You might struggle to find positive words, and that is why I am here. I know you; I see you. You are smart, funny, really kind, and a good friend. You notice the small stuff, and you make people feel special. So add that to your list and keep building.

Do not hold back or be afraid that someone will judge you. You don't have to show anyone these positive affirmations. These positive affirmations are your new weapon to keep the rocks out of your backpack. Then, look at that list, post it on your wall or mirror, or put it under your pillow. Repeat the strengths and qualities that you have.

You have survived the bullying. Now is the time to rebuild yourself. Each day, repeat the "I am" statements until you own them; you believe them at your core. Let me help you. Here are my top ten:

1. I am strong. I am not a victim.
2. I am smart.
3. I love myself.
4. I am good enough.
5. I am helpful.
6. I stand up for myself and others.
7. I am no longer carrying rocks that hurt me.
8. I am forgiving.
9. I am funny. I use humor as my armor.
10. I am a leader.

I know you can do it! I believe in you!

Sending you love, strength, and lots of positivity,

The Bully Teacher

Stop and Think

"I am" Statements

As parents, we want to motivate our children and make them strong, but sometimes, we forget to fuel them with the ammunition they need to be strong. Positive affirmations are the best way to encourage our children and keep them emotionally balanced. Often, we get stuck in routines—thinking about healthy food, homework, and after-school activities—but we do not make time for the emotional welfare of our kids. We don't do it on purpose. We are so busy, we are in our heads, we have high hopes for our kids, and we forget to ask them what they need to feel safe and secure.

Some of us were raised to repress our emotions and not to think about how we should feel. We were raised to work hard, to fight, to build something better for our children, but we don't see our children's dreams or visions. To some of us, thinking about emotions and learning how to communicate and talk about our emotions is unfamiliar territory, an unknown land.

Some of us were raised to believe that feelings don't matter, or that we don't have time for feelings. We might have heard had a lot of: "Stop crying"; "Don't show your emotions in public"; "Don't get too excited, happy, or joyful"; "Why are you so sensitive?" The list goes on. Some of us are wired to work hard and play hard. Some of us are wired to stuff our emotions and just make sure our homes are perfect. Some of us are wired never to show our weaknesses and not to trust anyone. Some of us are wired to hide all our emotions in drugs, alcohol, and food.

We just hide all of what we feel and pretend we are not affected. We numb, we forget, we push down all those big emotions. The problem is that our children feel those emotions, too. They feel the stress, the loneliness, the sadness we feel. We all live under the same roof. No matter how hard we try to protect our children, they feel our pain. And when it rains, it pours.

Sometimes, we watch our kids have emotions that we were never granted. We might feel uncomfortable and be dismissive: "Stop being so dramatic," or "Don't be so sensitive." "It is not a big deal; get over it." These statements can hold a lot of weight and power. They can be really hurtful.

We can't push our own beliefs or emotions onto our kids. We need to learn to better understand our children and to help them process their feelings. When we understand the power of affirmations, we can shift our home environment.

When our children have bad days or are sad, positive affirmations or gratitude statements are key to helping them pivot into a better mood. The best time to use positive affirmations is in the morning, when a child first wakes up and at night, before they fall asleep. They get to wake up thinking they are special, and they go to bed feeling loved.

We can try positive affirmations out on ourselves before we attempt them on our children. If we set our alarms to something that jazzes us up, something that gets us out of bed, we wake up thinking that this will be a great day. It changes our whole perspective, because it is a new day, filled with hope and opportunity. Nothing is FAN (forever, always, and never); it will all pass. Even the worst pain or trauma shall pass. Time heals all wounds, but we need to let time run its course and process our pain. Once we have processed the pain, we can accept joy, positivity, love, hope, and support.

As part of our work with positive affirmations, we need to work on feeling gratitude. Gratitude is a muscle that we need to exercise more and more in our home. Gratitude builds resilience and helps us pivot to find what brings us comfort and joy. Working with at-risk youth is often difficult; gratitude is hard, and resistance builds up. Working with privileged kids, gratitude is also hard. How funny it is to see that we all struggle to see what we are grateful for, to find what we truly appreciate.

We should think about how we set our minds when we wake up and how we set our day as our feet touch the ground. Most of us wake up feeling grumpy or unsure. We should feel encouraged to be outside that norm and to tell our children all the wonderful things we love about them right when they wake up, before any negative thoughts flow into their minds. Working parents who are not at home in the morning can write notes on the fridge or the mirror or leave notes on a child's bed. They can even leave them messages on Alexa or Google. There is always a way to leave positive affirmations. We should never overlook this process. It is the most critical part of building self-esteem, resilience, and more love in our lives.

We might not believe these positive thoughts, but we should think about how we would feel if we could focus on the best of ourselves every day. Positive affirmations are game changers. We promise there will be no regrets when we think about how great and amazing we can be each and every single day!

Below are some examples of positive affirmations:
- I am strong.
- I am brave.
- I am a dreamer.
- I got this.
- I am going to rock this day.
- I am a superhero.
- I am not afraid of my monsters.
- I have my power.
- I am beautiful.
- I am glorious.
- I am smart.
- I am powerful.
- I am cool.
- I like my style.
- I am going to make it a great day.
- I love me.
- I am an athlete.
- I can read.
- I am good at writing.
- I am good at dance.
- I am good at soccer.
- I am loved.
- I am doing the best I can.
- I am trying my best.
- I am in control of my emotions.
- I am good enough.
- I am worthy.

If we struggle with these affirmations, we can try these gratitude statements first:
- I am grateful for my health.
- I am grateful for the food in my fridge.
- I am grateful for my life.
- I am grateful for my bed.
- I am grateful for having a loving home.
- I am grateful for having food on my table.
- I am grateful for my home.
- I am grateful for my room.
- I am grateful for having money this week.
- I am grateful for my job.
- I am grateful for my family.
- I am grateful for my grandma.
- I am grateful for my dog or cat.
- I am grateful to have clothes.
- I am grateful to have my cousins.
- I am grateful to have breakfast at school.
- I am grateful to be at school.

Below are some more gratitude statements; these might be a little difficult to read. They are some statements from the children in our programs. Some might be dark, but they are real, and we want to share how they view their world:

- I am grateful to have a family.
- I am grateful to have food on my table.
- I am grateful for my life.
- I am grateful for my nanny.
- I am grateful for my neighbor.
- I am grateful that my family is safe. I am afraid of ICE.
- I am grateful we have money to keep our gas on.
- I am grateful for my internet.
- I am grateful for a roof over my head.
- I am grateful to have a teacher that cares about me.
- I am grateful to have dinner tonight.
- I am grateful that my parents are not fighting.
- I am grateful my dad stopped touching me.
- I am grateful my mom is sober.
- I am grateful my dad left.
- I am grateful to sleep in a home where I am loved.
- I am grateful to not be homeless.
- I am grateful for sports.
- I am grateful I am not scared to talk about what happened to me.
- I am grateful I left my abusive home.
- I am grateful my mom saw her boyfriend beat me.
- I am grateful the librarian saw the boy was touching me.

- I am grateful I did not kill myself.
- I am grateful my friend told a teacher I was cutting.
- I am grateful I have an aunt that would support me.
- I am grateful I got a second chance.
- I am grateful that I survived my suicide attempt.
- I am grateful for my counselor. She saw I needed help.
- I am grateful for my classmate helping me.
- I am grateful for my principal.
- I am grateful for my teacher.
- I am grateful for Bulldog.

These are all statements from elementary school. Let's eradicate all fear with honest conversations. Parenting is hard, and being a teacher can be brutal at times, so we should review what our children say in their gratitude statements and have a conversation about whatever monsters might be scaring them. We can talk about shifting the paradigm to bring more and more positivity into their lives. We need more love.

We must find what chains our children down and what makes them scared and find their strengths. Emotions are critical, and children's feelings rule their intelligence. We must work on building our kids up, one positive affirmation at a time!

Chapter 11: Parent Divorce and Summer Camp

Dear Bully,

I am constantly left out and bullied at camp. I am smaller and it is hard for me to do some of the activities. You started the cycle a few years ago. I watched you exclude me and I didn't understand why. It happens every year I have to come to this stupid camp. I hate it. It is a family tradition. Why do I have to follow in my parents' footsteps? My parents are divorced now, so why does it even matter. This is the only tradition they push on me. I don't even know what family means anymore. I am alone in my own home, I am alone at this camp.

What did I ever do to you? Now, I am excluded or picked on as soon as the first day of camp starts. I hate camp. I hate my life. I have to come back every year. I wish I could disappear. What is wrong with my parents? Why do they care about this camp?

Camp Hater

Dear Victim,

At my summer camp a few years ago I left you out at a lot of things because you annoyed me. Your family is so annoying and always putting people down. Your dad acts like he runs the world. Then when I saw you, sitting alone, you reminded me of me. I saw myself. My dad is a piece of shit. He cheated on my mom and left her. We went from living in our huge home to a two bedroom apartment. I am so ashamed of my life.

I am sorry for what I started. I have felt bad watching you being left out, and eventually you stopped trying to hang out. I saw you, and I felt so much guilt. It turned to anger like why can't you just be normal?

I learned that I am embarrassed of myself sometimes. Why can't I be normal? Why can't my parents stop fighting about money and see me? I don't care about money or cars, I feel like I am stuck being torn between them. They use me as bait. I know it and I use it to get what I want. I use my words to hurt people like I have been hurt.

I wish I can invite you in and tell you all this, is it too late to say I am sorry? Our parents hate each other. I don't know why. Who can I talk to about this? I seem like a cry baby.

I saw people bullying you the other day. I stood there, I felt bad. It haunts me at night. I replay what happened. I started it and it was not your fault. I was dealing with my parents divorce and I was so mad. I turned and saw you. You were the only one at camp that knew my situation. Torn that I started all this. How do I go back and fix this? I feel horrible, but I stand there and laugh at you.

The Bully

Stop and Think

Divorce and Bullying

In our work, we encounter a lot of divorce in elementary school, and although it is common, it is still painful. In a divorce, a child is being ripped from the home. The new situation might be better, but it is still a change. We always recommend therapy for children of divorce, but often, the parents would benefit from it, too. We must think about their pain as well. They made a vow, and it has been broken. We would love for parents to think about accountability versus blame. It is hard, and there are many painful feelings in a divorce, but no one is to blame. We must learn grace and appreciation for the other person.

Parents should forget about their pain for one second and look at their kids, who are also in pain; all they all want to be is perfect for their parents. Their home has been destroyed, and their parents must rebuild the new normal—find their new normal and make it better. Parents should try not to blame their spouses, because they will see later how that blame impacts middle school students. Kind adults and loving parents can put their differences aside in front of the kids. As non-divorce connoisseurs who are still human, we believe in love and know that it is important that parents not trash their significant others in front of their children. Parents' attitudes toward one another during a divorce have such huge impacts on the worlds of their children. Parents often have no idea about this effect. Sadly, their children have shown us the effect. As adults, we need to be more aware of how we impact our children.

Here are some statements we heard from elementary school kids dealing with divorced parents. Some statements are direct quotes from what their parents said to or about one another.
"Dad left for a new family."
"Mom is a gold-digger."
"Mom is a crack whore."
"Dad met someone else and does not care about us."
"Mom is in jail."
"Mom is a bitch."
"I can't see you. Mom won't let me."
"Your mom is a drunk whore. She ruined our marriage."
"Dad left us because it was too much."
"Mom is taking me for all my money, so I have to leave for a while."
"Dad cheated on Mom. He doesn't care about us."
"Mom spends too much money. I need to teach her a lesson."
"Dad works a lot, and he does not have time for me."
"Your mom never loved you."
"Dad left you. You were a mistake."
"He left us because of you."
"If you were a better kid, he would have stayed."
"Your mom changed the day you were born. She never was herself.
"Mom couldn't handle it. She left."
"You are the reason Mom left."
"You are the reason Dad left."

These statements might have been difficult to stomach, but they are real and might not be too different from something we have heard or said. Sometimes, we need to think about how our words are like swords that can puncture the hearts of others. We should think of new statements that fuel healing and connections.

Here are a few statements that parents can use to replace more painful ones:

"Dad and I are getting a divorce. We want you to live in a happy and healthy home. We have so much respect for each other and will always love each other. We need to separate to grow and be happy. You're the best part of both of us, and we love you so much."

"Mom and I grew apart. We don't see eye to eye. We're really sad about this, but we know that separation is the best for you and us. We love you so much, and we want what would be best for you."

"We've both changed, and we're struggling to understand each other and communicate. Our fights and behaviors are not healthy. We want you to see what it is to have happy, loving, and supportive homes. We can learn to rebuild."

"We've both made mistakes, and we have to move on and forgive each other. To do that, we both need space from each other. We're doing our best, and we're sorry for any pain we've caused."

Chapter 12: Conflict Resolution for Hitting Behaviors

Dear Bulldog,

Last year, I was friends with this girl she was fine but then she started to hit me and push me at random times when we would line up for school. One time, I was standing in line and she pushed me to the ground. It really hurt me. Then I told someone and she stopped, but started doing to other people what she did to me.

Pushed Down

Dear Pushed Down,

I am sorry that someone would intentionally push and hit you. I applaud you for standing up for yourself. You were very brave to tell someone what was going on. When we report bad behavior, it often stops, but in your case, the classmate moved on to new targets.

I am sad that this is now happening to your other classmates. Is there any piece of advice you can give them in making this stop for them?

I encourage you to talk to the other students and help them use the strategy that you used—like telling a teacher or asking the student to stop. Maybe you could ask the teacher to have a one-on-one with the student to find out why she is pushing. She must have some anger or something that is hurting her and that makes her need to push people.

If you feel brave enough, you can also tell the bully about how you felt about being pushed. Your words are powerful; use them for good and to stick up for yourself and others. Sometimes, having scary or uncomfortable conversations is the way to create change.

Sending you Love and Positivity,

The Bully Teacher

Stop and Think
Conflict Resolution

We see pushing in line and shoving more often in early elementary. We need to address personal space and appropriate play. Children don't always understand personal space or why it is important to keep their hands to themselves as they line up. In early elementary, children often struggle with miscommunication, arguments, disagreements, and fights. Often, students who might exhibit more aggression or anger resort to hitting and pushing when faced with negative emotions. It is frustrating and often infuriating when parents hear that their kid is being pushed, hit, or shoved at school.

We need to teach children about their body space, about how to value personal space, and about how to create boundaries so that when they are so close together, they can reduce conflict and understand the effect of not respecting personal space.

In most cases, the children doing the pushing and shoving need intervention to better process their emotions. Such intervention can be a quick fix if done appropriately.

Below are some strategies for educators and administrators. We highly recommend that parents not engage with another child without the permission of that child's parents. We have often seen situations go sour when parents confront a child not their own.

Strategies to Manage Pushing and Shoving:

1. Take the pushing child out of the situation and find a quiet, open, and safe place to talk to the child. This place might be the library, a quiet corner, an empty lunch room, a deserted hallway, or any place where the child can easily regain their composure.
2. Get on their level. Sit down with them, and use open body language to be calm, compassionate, and welcoming. This means not crossing your arms, not standing over the child, and not having your hands on your hips and looking down at the child.
3. Open the conversation with clear expectations and desired outcomes: "Vivian, I want to spend this time listening and see how I can better support you. I want to create a safe and trusting space, where you can share with me what is going on. I care about you and your well-being. I have been concerned. You seem to be dealing with a lot. That makes me sad, and I want to be here for you." Frame the conversation to fit your teaching or leadership style, but make sure you talk about safety, trust, openness, concern, and support. The child needs to feel safe to talk.
4. Open up the conversation with inquisitive, compassionate questions to gain more insight. Your goal is to get to the root of the pushing, hitting, or shoving. Ask questions that will guide you to some great insight:

    o "Can you tell me more about what is happening when you line up?"

- "It seems like in the morning lineup, you get angry or upset. What happens?"

- "Walk me through your morning routine from home to school. I want to hear how you start out your day."

- "Tell me about your classmates. Who are your friends?"

- "What makes you angry or irritates you in the morning?"

- "What can I do to better support you during lineup?"

- "What can you do to help yourself during lineup?"

- "When you get mad, how do you react?"

- "When you get mad, what are you thinking?"

5. Ask more about what the child wants and how you can support them. Let them feel empowered to make decisions and change the situation.
6. Switch it up by asking about how they think their classmates may feel when pushed and shoved. Ask them about a time someone else pushed or shoved them. Identify the emotions they felt and apply those ideas to their current situation.
7. Talk about apologies and how to deliver a good apology. Go over what is a good apology and the benefits of apologizing. Talk about sincerity and the idea that owning up to their mistakes makes them stronger.
8. Create new morning habits during lineup that fuel connection. These habits are helpful in replacing hitting and shoving behaviors. Give the child options to replace their negative behavior.
9. Reinforce the new habits with incentives and positive feedback. Take the time to connect to the student and reinforce the new habit with positive words. Give them a reward after a certain amount of time; for example, in two weeks, they might get a celebratory sticker or free time. You might give them some incentive to try every day to replace the old habit.
10. Follow up and make room for mistakes. There will be days where the child might resort to pushing again. These are days when they need the most help and guidance. Go over what happened and how to make it better. Take the time to talk, not shame the child.

This conversation is about discovering the emotions and thoughts behind the physical behavior. When we get to the root, we can help find new thoughts and behaviors to replace the hitting. This discovery process takes a little time and commitment, but when we have done it and followed up, we have helped children manage their emotions and better connect with their classmates.

Chapter 13: New Kid-New School Drama

Dear Bulldog,

It was the first day at my new school and I saw a lot of people looking at me and turning away to whisper to their friends. This made me feel scared and insecure. In the classroom, no one immediately came up to me and they all had this look on their faces like they were seeing a monster. I'm tall so that is how I see myself, I felt as if I was a monster and they could not escape from me. I didn't make many friends that year and this made me feel sad and that something was wrong with me. This is why I'm so quiet and keep to myself. I wish I had more confidence.

New Girl

Dear New Girl,

I am sorry that you have felt this way. It must be scary to come to a new school and not know anyone. I'm a tall girl as well, and I remember being your age and feeling different from others. You're not alone. I know what it is to be the tallest girl in your class when you are younger. The first thing I want to tell you is that you are beautiful.

Being tall is a wonderful thing. Do you know that when someone is tall, they are automatically perceived as being authoritative and confident because many leadership positions are occupied by tall people? It's true! The great chef Julia Child once said, "Being tall is an advantage, especially in business. People will always remember you." You are wonderful just the way you are.

It can be hard to gain confidence, but I think if you start thinking of the positives, you can really shift your perspective. Think about all the celebrities and athletes who are tall. Google them and read their stories. Watch movies or read books about tall women. *Tall Girl* from Netflix might be a good one to start with. Find resources, movies, and books, and surround yourself with support. Write down all the reasons it might be helpful to be tall. Here is my list:
- I can reach higher than most, so I can help my mom get stuff on the higher shelves.
- I have helped a lot of kids who were bullied, because when I approach the bullies, they think I am older.
- I am good at jumping high and am a faster runner.
- I don't have to wear uncomfortable shoes to look taller.
- I get to go on all the roller coasters.
- My siblings think I am strong and that I protect them.

Ask your parents or friends to help you create the list.

Take a few post-its and post some positive words about yourself on your bathroom mirror or behind your door. State them every morning as you get ready for school or to go out. At first, these affirmations might not feel true, but with constant repetition, your mind will start to believe what you are saying. It is all about how you perceive yourself. Now I love being tall and strong. I want you to feel the same way I do, every day!

Best,

The Bully Teacher

Stop and Think

Building Self-Esteem at a Young Age

During many of our programs, we have spoken to students and find that they feel a lack of confidence. Although we want to focus on their brains, they mostly focus on what people can see about them.

Children may think negatively about themselves and not understand how others truly see them. They focus on what makes them different versus what connects them to their peers—what makes them weak or ugly, versus what makes them strong and beautiful. These perceived negatives could be race, gender identity, religion, hair, height, weight, glasses, noses, eyes, a visible disability, and many other characteristics.
Other children turn their fear of differences against others, target and making fun of them.

It is important to celebrate our differences and our strengths and to find commonalities among one another. We also must help children embrace their inner and outer beauty. If they believe they are beautiful and powerful, despite being different, other people see those qualities, too. They have to start thinking more about the positive and really embrace themselves. Ownership of who they are is so important for healthy emotional growth.

parents can do something as small as leaving their child a note in their bag with a positive statement to help change their mindset about themselves for the day.

Parents can leave a positive affirmation such as:

"You're so brave," if their children are facing something challenging that day.
"Your voice matters," if their children are fearful of speaking up in class.
"I love your outfit, your hair, or the way you decorated your backpack."
"You're beautiful." This is such an important statement. (Beauty is more than just what we see in the mirror.)
"I love your singing. It brightens my day."
"You have the most beautiful eyes. They are wise and give me so much hope."
"Your smile brightens up a room."
"Your skin is glowing."
"I love your strong, athletic body."
"You're so strong and fit."

"You're agile."
"Your hair looks beautiful."

We can go on and on about addressing a child's strong, beautiful physical aspects. Some parents are infuriated that we recommend using the words "beautiful" or "pretty" to describe their children. These parents don't want to focus on their children's physical appearances. However, we will fight tooth and nail about this topic, because the children themselves all focus on their physical appearances; they focus on them all the time. They compare themselves to their peers, to the characters on shows they watch, and to the YouTube celebrities they admire. We believe in repeatedly mentioning a child's positive physical qualities to them. We can't escape our culture of beauty, but we can put a new spin on physical appearance to give children the social emotional resilience to have high self-esteem.

Our children need to know that they are loved for all their special qualities on the inside and outside. They need to know what makes them sparkly on the outside. They want parents to comment on their style and their appearance and for their parents to show them who they are. Parents can't ignore those desires.

We remember a mother telling us, "I would appreciate you not calling my daughter pretty, but talked about how smart she is." We responded with: "Why does it have to be 'either/or?' Why can't it be 'and?'" A person can be smart and beautiful. A person can be a math genius and pretty. A person can be an excellent ballerina and handsome. We need to stop with the "either/or" and open our vocabulary to "and," because over time, ignoring a child's outer beauty can have a negative impact on them.

We have worked with thousands of children over the years. If we ignore their physical appearances, they often feel ugly or invisible. We have heard the following statements:

- "My mom has never told me I'm beautiful."
- "My mom only focuses on my academics. She doesn't even know my style."
- "My dad is afraid to give me a compliment. He thinks it will give me the wrong impression about myself."
- "I don't feel seen."
- "I'm invisible."
- "I'm ugly."
- "I'm fat."
- "I'm too skinny."
- "I hate my hair."
- "I hate my skin."
- "My face is so ugly."
- "I'm disgusting."
- "I know I'm smart, but all I want is to be pretty."

Children think about their appearances, and their appearances matter to them. We must tell them they are beautiful, especially at a young age. We don't want to raise pompous children. We want to raise confident children with high self-esteems. Pompous children have a lack of self-esteem; confident children are leaders and find beauty and joy without harming others.

We should ask our kids what types of compliments they like and what they like about themselves. We can tell them when they look good and compliment them more often. We want them to model this self-esteem and believe in those compliments, so we must go back to the "I am" statements, which help build their confidence.

Teaching children "I am" statements requires repetition and consistency. Children should repeat some "I am" statements with their parents once a day: "I am smart"; "I am capable"; "I am beautiful." And parents should not forget to help set the example by doing this exercise, too! We recommend doing the exercises first thing in the morning.

For children with physical appearances that might be different from those of their classmates, parents can help them find a mentor or a group of people who are like them. We have unlimited access to knowledge at our disposal and should use it to find support to help our children feel connected and understood.

Reflection Checkpoint

In this section, we have reviewed many different forms of bullying and negative social conflict. We would like to recap our Stop and Think sections to bring all the strategies and ideas full circle. To prevent bullying, we need to work on teaching our children about friendship, appropriate play, exclusion, and being mean. We also need to reflect on what goes on in our homes and how it might impact our child. By being more aware of how we communicate, feel, and act, we can often stop arguments or drama from escalating in our own homes.

A child who knows how to regulate their emotions and process them is less likely to bully or hit other children. We encourage all of our educators and parents to bridge the gap between school and home. As parents, keeping our judgment, opinions, and criticism to ourselves when it comes to our children's teachers is important. We have seen an increase in disrespect between parents and teachers, but as parents, we must support our teachers. We can agree to disagree with our children's teachers or take our concerns directly to the teacher, not discuss them at the dinner table. Our children retain all this information, so if we badmouth the teacher, the child thinks they can follow suit, negatively impacting classroom management.

Classroom management and bullying prevention go hand and hand. When children have clear expectations, boundaries, and rules to follow, they are less likely to attack each other during structured, regulated time. When educators are structured, consistent, and repetitive, they help students with transitions and learning. We have worked in thousands of classrooms, and some of them are overcrowded (up to 35 children in one class). With overcrowding come a great deal of challenges in classroom management. But building social emotional skills at a young age and being consistent in the lessons help with classroom management.

We also want to re-emphasize the FAN Syndrome. Teaching our children about change and reiterating that nothing lasts forever creates a powerful mindset. We should pay attention to our children when they start to FAN and bring their focus back to the specific incident. We want to teach our children to overcome challenges, not accumulate resentment. By eliminating FAN words as much as we can, we start to break up negative patterns of thinking.

The importance of the tattling syndrome also needs to be reiterated. We need to teach our children to stand up and speak out for themselves. Children are so afraid to tell and be labeled as snitches that they suffer for years in silence. This silence can destroy their inner selves and create a series of negative behaviors. We must talk about the difference between tattling and telling and teach our children to be advocates for themselves and others. We can use visuals and fun analogies so that children can imagine telling or saying something to stop bullying. It is our job to advocate for our children, but we also need to teach them how to advocate for themselves.

Apologizing and forgiving should be everyone's new mantra! We want to be open and willing to accept our wrongdoing, to apologize with sincerity, to eliminate blame, and to forgive each other more. When we take our egos out of the equation and really evaluate a situation, we have room to process our emotions. By forgiving more, we let go of resentment and pain, and become freer. Feeling emotionally free is joyous and liberating. We all need a little more sunshine and joy in our lives.

We also want to revisit the topic of building self-esteem at a young age, focusing on our children's strengths and physical traits. By sending positive affirmations inward and outward, we help our children feel more confident and self-assured. When we don't use enough positive affirmations, our children might struggle with their self-worth or feel the need to validate themselves through their accomplishments or judge themselves based on their failures. We see a lot of attention-seeking behaviors from children with low self-esteem. Children always want to feel seen, heard, and connected. They want to feel appreciated, loved, and supported. By teaching them how to love themselves, we encourage them to be more resilient and confident. They then have less of a need to seek outside sources of validation. We should start those positive affirmations today!

We also hope parents and teachers will review the various types of teasing with their children. Understanding the difference between good, bad, and unintentional mean teasing really helps children better understand social boundaries. This understanding can help prevent arguments, drama, and bullying. Often, rumors or teasing result in hurt feelings. Conflict escalates from miscommunications and hurt feelings. We must take the time to teach our children about teasing and conflict, giving them a leg up when entering middle school.

In closing, we share an excellent strategy from a wonderful mom and amazing social worker who helps her four kids build kindness at home. She was tired of what she called the "Lunch Room Drama," so she came up with a strategy to combat it. She taught us her trick, and we want readers to try it. It is called the "Lunch and Learn" strategy. After school, this mom holds a family meeting and asks her kids one question: "Who did you sit with at lunch, and what did you learn?" If one of her kids sits with a new kid, remembers their name, and shares what they learned about their new friend, she *might* offer up a prize.

The catch is that they never know if there is a prize or reward, so each day, they try hard to meet new friends and learn about their classmates. They remember names and ask questions that build connections. Lunch and Learn has become a family routine.

I thought this was the coolest strategy to learn what is going on during free time and see how her kids are connecting with their peers. It is amazing! This mom's children have developed a plethora of friends, and since they are a crew of four in a small school, other kids have started following in their footsteps. Now, kids switch around to different groups of friends with an inclusive mindset. The prizes are the least important part of the activity, but the beautiful thing is that the prizes can be as simple as:
- Getting to use the iPad for fifteen more minutes.
- Spending quality time with mom.
- Picking the family movie.
- Staying up a little later on the weekends.
- Giving one chore away for the week.
- Getting a playdate.
- Picking a family activity on the weekends.
- Getting first dibs on dessert.
- Having a family dance party.

And the list can go on. Incentives can be powerful when used to build connections. These rewards might seem small, but to our children, they mean the world.

Middle and High School

If you thought the elementary school stories tugged at your heartstrings, the middle and high school ones will be even more challenging for you. In this section, the stories become more complex, and the problems are often more difficult or uncomfortable for parents to handle. After much consideration, we decided to pair middle school and high school together, because we noticed an inconsistent pattern in problems based on the maturity, socioeconomic background, and demographic backgrounds of the students.

Children face a variety of different problems, and the distances between the schools are not the only determinants of difference. Students at schools in Illinois, Indiana, Kentucky, and Florida face very different problems from one another, but we also see multiple disconnects between students at schools closer in proximity to one another, like those on the north and south side of Chicago. Some of the problems are unexpected, such as sixth graders being recruited for gangs, seventh graders experimenting with drugs, and eighth graders becoming sexually active.

But parents are the experts at raising their children. We want to give them the tools they need without putting children into a box that says, "This is where they should or should not be." Regardless of what timeline we have in our heads, children progress at a pace that matches their environment and self-development.

This section follows the same format as the last, with Areas of Focus and important definitions for each age group. We then move into the chapters and stories. We placed similar topics for middle and high school together; however, readers will see an indicator of what age group wrote each letter. Some chapters have two "Stop and Think" sections to tackle the issues in middle school and high school separately, as they may have different approaches.

Middle School

Area of Focus

We categorize middle school as sixth, seventh, and eighth grade. This age group goes through many transitions—changes in their bodies, moves to different schools, and the challenge of making new friends, all while learning to better understand social cues and constructs. Children are trying to understand how they fit into the world and who they connect with. They are finding new interests in sports, drama, band, orchestra, and beyond. Children have busier schedules, which increase the stress that they face. Children spend seven hours a day in school and two hours in after-school programs. Then, they go home and finish their homework and start preparing for the next day. They do a lot of moving, showing up, performing, focusing, and delivering before they finally get back to their homes—lots of doing and often time not enough processing.

Our children face stress, not only from their cramped schedules, but also from the new expectations and responsibilities placed on them at this age. In middle school, children experience so much change at once that it can be overwhelming. They are more conscious of their grades and their behaviors in the classroom, and they start to see the impact they have on their environments. They are more attuned with the performance expectations set by their parents and teachers. Students are stressed from the new conflicts and dramas that they face, as these impact their focus and performance. More intense conflicts naturally emerge, due to the complex, interwoven network of social interaction. In these grades, we see an increase in harmful conflict, both physical and psychological.

This is also the age where children become self-conscious and aware of their own self-esteem. They seek additional approval or validation from others and become more interested in romantic relationships. It is a confusing time, with a lot of unknowns and a wild variety of emotions. Children's moods often fluctuate, and they are more easily embarrassed. They want more privacy and crave more freedom.

Because children of this age crave being seen, they can easily use their need for attention or validation to exploit others or to overexpose themselves online. Some teens have different accounts on social media. They have public Instagram accounts and then Finstagram accounts. They have fake profiles and public ones. They put their public and private selves on the internet, to be seen by all.

At this age, children want to do things on their own. They are becoming teenagers, and they demand more freedom and less guidance. They want independence and control over their decisions. This is the time when they need the best navigation tools, but, as educators and parents, we need to learn how to guide from a distance and how to take the backseat as our children steer through complex social interactions. As parents and educators. we must give students the tools they need to navigate their world.

In our programs with this age group, we focus on how to address emotions—how to identify, understand, and process them. We help children build connections so that they will feel empathy and understand that their actions have an impact on others. We work on letting go of the past and building their ideal selves. We work on handling conflict, managing stress, and how to efficiently communicate with others.

Definitions to Know

Drama: Rumors, gossip, and teasing between individuals or groups in conflict situations. Drama is not bullying, as there is not a differentiation in power between individuals. With drama, the person being targeted also retaliates or fights back.

Teasing: When one person makes fun of another. As we saw in the elementary school section, there are different types of teasing: good teasing, bad teasing, and unintentional teasing.

- Good Teasing: The individual feels liked by the teaser, and the teasing is done with good intentions, to show affection.
- Unintentional Mean Teasing or Roasting: The teaser does not know the individual is hurt or dismisses his/her feelings because the teaser does not understand them.
- Bad or Mean Teasing: The teasing is done to make the individual feel bad and to hurt the other person. When the individual asks the teaser to stop, the teaser responds, "Don't be a baby", "You're so sensitive", "Just kidding", or "It's a *joke*!" However, the teasing does not stop.

Gossip and rumors: When people share private or false information about an individual with the intent to spread that information.

High School

Area of Focus

The high school category includes ninth through twelfth grades. The young adults in this group often deal with all facets of identity, reputation, and expectations. We have seen a rise in self-esteem issues and stress as they relate to school, peer pressure, relationships, and sports. Teens feel pressure to perform and to be seen as being the best in the classroom and in their extracurricular activities. Sometimes they create this stress for themselves, and at other times, the stress appears as a result of maintaining an expectation set by their parents, peers, or coaches/teachers. Besides the people mentioned above, students feel pressure from the media, society, and peers, regarding alcohol, drugs, relationships, and sex. This stress affects their self-esteem and makes teenagers compare themselves to their classmates and make unrealistic comparisons to superstars or public figures (celebrities, Instagram/YouTube influencers, athletes, etc.)

Teenagers have a difficult time finding healthy ways to cope with stress. If someone feels bad about their body, they may develop an eating disorder, not a healthy lifestyle. If they are hurting, teens may resort to cutting or suicidal ideation instead of talking to someone about what's going on. Just like elementary and middle school students, high schoolers have a difficult time letting go of past mistakes and traumas.

Additionally, teenagers worry about creating a legacy—one that will stick after they leave high school. Simultaneously, they are trying to figure out what they are going to be beyond high school. "Will I go to college? Join the military? Help with my family? Learn a trade?" The choices are endless and seem monumental at this phase in their lives. Students feel as if they have to decide what to do for the rest of their lives when they are only eighteen years old.

Of course, drama associated with this age group also stems from jealousy, being misunderstood (confused and lonely), and defending a reputation (pride). When we reach the root causes of the drama, gossip, and rumors, we learn that it is often fueled by past or current assumptions. We have heard so many teens say, "Well, at first I didn't like you because of _____, but now we're friends." Teenagers often misunderstand one another's actions, which leads to increased conflict. Understandings comes from how they interpret words, how others treat them or see them, and how they interact with each other. We could say that judgment is at an all-time high during these years, and identity is easily defined by clicks or labels teenagers accumulate over the years.

Surprisingly, many high schoolers do not recognize their emotions, stressors, and other social emotional terminology. This lack of recognition only makes all of the above situations worse. Every year we are surprised by the number of high school students who do not know what a "stereotype" is. During our Bulldog sessions for teens, we focus on self- and social awareness, recognizing triggers and stressors, and tackling all of the above issues. Sometimes, our sessions get "derailed," as the students raise issues that are relevant and happening in the moment. In the moment is always the best time to handle a situation. If teens do not have a grip on themselves, then how are they going to maintain healthy relationships with others?

Definitions to Know

Stereotypes: The blanket beliefs that we assign to people of a certain group or clique. (Athletes are dumb or those in band are geeks.)
Self-Esteem: How people feel about themselves physically and mentally. Self-worth is tied to self-esteem.
Self-Awareness: How able someone is to understand their emotions, thoughts, and behaviors. Those with high self-awareness are better at regulating their emotions and have less emotional drive.
Social-Awareness: How attuned someone is to how their actions are perceived. It includes understanding social cues.
Reputation: The invisible label of how other people view someone. Reputation can be based on factual information or rumors/ gossip that others assume to be true.
Triggers: The words and/or actions of others or thoughts that take someone out of a moment and result in an emotional response or action.

Chapter 14: Stress and Anxiety and Bullying

Middle School Letter, 6th Grade

Dear Bully,

I don't understand why you pick on me. I try so hard to get the best grades. I am constantly nice to you. I love to share positive thoughts and be there for all my classmates. I don't know what your deal is with me. I am tired of being roasted by you. It is not my fault my parents have money, I can't control how involved my mom is at school, and I don't want to throw it in your face. I worked hard like since I was 4 to be a good gymnast. I practice 5 times a week. I do meets on the weekend, I never have down time. I don't hang out with my friends or go to parties like you. I am either practicing, competing, or doing homework. Calling me privileged and mocking me really hurts. It hurts my self-esteem. I don't want to be mean, but I don't know how to make you stop.

The Privileged Classmate

Dear Victim,

I'm sorry for making you feel bad, I get so annoyed sometimes. It seems like your life is perfect and you are throwing it in my face. I never had the opportunity to do sports or compete like you do. I come home and take care of my brother. My mom always works late and I have never met my dad. You come from a perfect family, so I make fun of you because I wish I had your life. I wish someone would call me privileged. You know I don't know if I will make it to graduation. I am constantly stressed about money. So seeing it come so easily to you pisses me off. I am sorry I hurt you and I wish deep down someday we could be friends.

The Bully

STOP AND THINK

Stress and Anxiety in Middle School

We have seen a dramatic rise in stress and anxiety in middle school. Ten years ago, when we first started our Bulldog programs, middle school was difficult, but not to the extent that it is now. It took us a while to figure out what was going on and how to tackle this new epidemic. Children in middle school now are stressed out and often pitted against one another. They compete with each other and are under enormous pressure to get good grades, make it into the best high schools, do their best in sports or after-school activities, and as they would put it, to be perfect. We have concluded that academic performance and technology (social media platforms) fuel some of this anxiety by keeping our children busy and constantly under an invisible lens of scrutiny that measures perfection. This lens allows critiques of a child's every move and pushes judgment before well-being, and it can be dangerous. The lens enables a lot of negative self-talk, criticism, and judgment, and it can fuel more risky behaviors.

Middle schoolers also deal with a great deal of change and contrast. Their bodies are changing, they have new interests, they might be confused about their sexual identities, and they are learning to navigate more complex relationship dynamics. As they progress from middle school to high school, interpersonal conflict rises, social dynamics change, and the need to fit in drives a lot of their behaviors. Between parental pressure, social pressure at school, and social media expectations, middle schoolers desire perfection. To them, being perfect means being the best at school, having the most likes or views on social media, and performing like a well-oiled machine. The problem is that they are not machines but children stuck between being teenagers and still wanting to be children.

They are learning from their social environment what is cool and what is lame. They are constantly collecting data about who they are and about what is acceptable in middle school. This is all a great deal to manage, and it becomes still more complicated with the addition of social emotional learning (SEL) and everything the middle school brain wants to explore.

At Bulldog, we emphasize that SEL is not an "either/or" but a solution to manage all these big emotions—confusion, stress, anxiety, sadness, anger, embarrassment, shame, guilt, and the list goes on. These big emotions come with big reactions, and we want to help our children find balance by working on processing these emotions.

We have found that one stressor we often overlook is parental pressure. At this time in their lives, the children's need to please their parents is at an all-time high. They want to be the best, to be loved and valued, and they each want to be the perfect child. In some instances, they seek perfection through grades or sports; in others, they seek perfection by being the toughest or the most popular. We have found that kids in middle school are extremely fearful, or even terrified, of disappointing their parents or of making any kind of mistake.

From our perspective, this need for perfection must be addressed. Children fear that if they are not perfect or high-performing, they won't be loved. It is as though they fear that their parents' love is conditional. As we all know, that crazy thinking needs to be corrected in our children. How do we overcome this miscommunication and this fear of not being loved enough? What has happened to make our kids feel conditionally loved?

Conditional love means that if a child fails, struggles, loses, or gets caught for something serious, their parents will not love them anymore. We have seen students go to extreme measures to lie, hide, or blame others in order to remain in their parents' good graces.

As parents, we need to constantly repeat and share with our children how much we love them. We need to focus on their strengths more than on their accomplishments. We need to help them cope with their stress and anxiety. We need to stop dismissing their emotions or fears, because these emotions are real to them. Drama in middle school is at an all-time high. Every day, we hear new stories:

- Lily didn't want to talk to me today. She's mad at me, and I don't know why.
- Bobby pushed me and then laughed at me.
- They won't stop staring at me.
- My friends didn't save a seat for me at lunch. I had to sit alone. I felt everyone was looking at me.
- I know they're talking about me.
- So I can't be friends with so-and-so, because…
- Isabella is always laughing at me.
- Emma spread rumors about me.
- Abigail says I'm needy, and she doesn't want to hang out with me anymore.

The drama of these children is real, and it hurts them. Teasing and exclusion is painful. It adds a level of stress to their already stressful lives, so we want to address these social conflicts and reduce their stress. As parents, it is hard to listen to the same story over and over. We just want to say, "Layla, stop feeding into it. Just ignore them!" It is not that easy. We push our strategies onto our kids without realizing that these strategies will not work, or perhaps, our child does not know how to use the strategies that seem so simple to us.

In our parent trainings, we talk about teaching children to "do their best" and not "be the best." These quotes describe two different frameworks and outcomes. Being the best means being number one, competing to get to the top, and winning at all costs. It is about a child's being; it is about them as a person, and there is a great deal of pressure to *be the best*. If a child can't be the best, then they feel as though they lose part of their identity. Over time, children who follow the framework of being the best put pressure on their own performances and actions, and often build unrealistic expectations. On the other hand, doing their best means trying hard, applying themselves, being present, and challenging themselves. It is action-directed; it is a behavior, and behavior can be changed.

Chapter 15: Teasing and Roasting

Middle School Letter, 7th Grade: Unintentional Teasing and Roasting

Dear Bully,

I know you say the things you say in a joking way, but it really hurts my feelings. I am starting to believe that I am the things you call me. It's really hard for me to tell you to stop, you don't have any idea that I'm getting hurt and annoyed by your roasting. You have stopped saying these things to me lately, because now you are picking on another person. I really don't like how you make other people feel.

Over Roasted

Dear Victim,

Roasting is my thing. It is what I am good at and it is easy for me. I know I cross the line, but I can't help myself. I am funny. It is the one thing I am good at. The one thing that I have for myself. I make people laugh. I am not a good athlete, I am not a good student, I am not good with sitting down and listening, and I have an attitude. I know what people say behind my back. He is dumb, stupid, slow, special, and the list goes on. When I use humor, I feel like myself. Sometimes, more often than others, I am making jokes and in a bad mood, so I roast people to feel better about myself. It works, not in a way that I feel good for a long time. But in that moment teasing someone else to get a laugh gives me a release, like I can breath, and I think to myself, I am not such a dummy, if I can put him down and there is no comeback. I kind of don't understand why everyone thinks I am dumb. I am never chosen as a lead, mentor, tutor, or helper. The teacher rolls her eyes when I ask, so I resort to being the class clown. It works for me. I think to myself "screw all of you, I am not dumb." I am sorry for hurting you. You are nice to me and I turned on you. It has been hard to adjust to middle school, I apologize for saying all those mean things.

The Bully

Middle School Letter, 6th Grade: Roasting and Mean Teasing

Dear Bully,

I don't understand your constant need to tease and harass me because of who I hang out with. You know I have no romantic interest in anyone, so please stop with the frequent "jokes" that I like this person or that person. It's immature and it really hurts. Please stop harassing me about "who I like" even when you know I don't "like" anybody. You are only hurting me and others with those "jokes."

I'm tired of the drama.

Teased and Tired

Dear Teased and Tired,

I am sorry that this is happening to you. I hope it felt good to write about it. It sounds like you are going through a difficult time with rumors and gossip. It seems like the bully's comments and rumors about who you like hurt you. They would hurt me, too. It is hard to control what people say about us, but I would recommend you try not to let it get to you. They are looking for an emotional reaction to get you going. Here are a few suggestions:

1- When you hear about the rumors, laugh them off and say, "Isn't this getting old?" Then, change the subject with your friends.

2- Confront the bully. Ask them why they are spreading rumors. Make sure you don't confront them in front of everyone; do it one-on-one. If you have the courage, share how much the "jokes" hurt you. Tell the person that they really hurt you. Showing them your perspective can help create connections. They might really think they are being funny, but once they know that they are hurting you, they might stop. Sometimes, in middle school, we don't realize we are hurting others, and we struggle with knowing when a joke has gone too far.

3- Have no emotional response. If you can act like the "jokes" really do not bother you, the bully will have no more ammunition. You have taken their power away. To get to a place of no emotional response, you need to really train your brain. Use deep breathing and repeat any mantras to yourself. Below are some examples:

"This isn't about me. He's looking to irritate me, and I won't let his comments get to me."
"I choose kindness over hate."
"I won't react to them. It's not worth my time."
"I won't get involved in the drama. I'm too busy to get sucked in."
"I choose my happiness over their rumors. I am worthy."

Find a mantra or something you can repeat in your head to help you.

We know that this behavior can be annoying, especially if your peers respond or others start to think that you like them and then start teasing you. It is a real mess. It can be infuriating, embarrassing, and stressful. Be strong, and don't engage with an emotionally driven response. Put up a positive wall. (Let positive thoughts fill your brain, so there is no room for drama.) Use these happy thoughts or surround yourself with positive people. This way, the words don't impact your happiness, and the person will stop.

You totally got this, and we are here for you.

Sending you love and positivity,

The Bully Teacher

Middle School Letter, 7th Grade: Roasting Intent Versus Impact

Dear Victim,

I can't stop thinking about you. I know I call you Drama Queen and it irritates you. I am the class clown and the jokester of 7th grade. I wish I could talk to you, but I get so shy. It is easier for me to make fun of you then just talk to you. I can see that sometimes my jokes go too far, but I get caught up in the crowd and I just want to make people laugh. It is easy to get you going. I make stuff up to get your attention, then you freak out and I keep going. I am sorry.

The Roaster

Dear Roaster,

We can see you that target her, and we know that you just want to be funny. The thing is that you are really hurting her feelings. You make fun of the way she talks and dresses, and other physical attributes that she can't control. She already has high anxiety, and your constant roasting is harmful to her.

You might think it is funny, but she goes home at night and questions her worth. She is becoming more and more self-conscious and fearful that everyone thinks the things you make fun of her for. You start out with good teasing (with the intent to get a laugh and build connections), but it quickly turns into unintentional mean teasing (with no intent to harm but the person being teased gets hurt). It is like you don't understand that there is a line between joking, roasting, and bullying.

We can ask you to stop, the school can give you consequences for not changing your behavior, or the counselors can call your parents. Honestly, we don't think any of these solutions will work. We would like you to think about the following questions:

What type of person do you want to be seen as?
Do you want to be seen as a bully—a mean person who people fear?
Do you want to have on your conscience the fact that you are hurting one of your classmates?
Do you want to be seen as a person who hurts others to gain social status?
Is this the legacy you want to leave?
Do you want your parents to think of you as a mean child?

We don't think you want to be seen like this, we don't think you want to be labeled as a bully, and we don't think you want to intentionally harm someone else.

You don't want to go to bed at night, thinking that you hurt someone so bad—that you are the reason they are crying themselves to sleep.

To have that on your conscience is heavy. It is not worth it.

Use your humor for good. Make fun of yourself sometimes or start working on jokes about things that don't relate to your peers. You are a leader, and you have a really great sense of humor. Would you like to leave a legacy of being the funniest and nicest middle school leader? That would really be a way to leave the school on a high note.

We leave you with this: Be the person whom the first and second graders look up to. Be the student who can turn sadness into laughter or change the course of someone's day for the positive by using your humor.

Sending you love and positivity,

The Bully Teacher

Stop and Think

Good Teasing, Roasting, and Bad/Mead Teasing
Once children typically hit middle school, they have a plethora of new words and social skills and a better understanding of sarcasm. They are still trying to figure out different emotions and how to socially interact to feel connected and accepted. Teasing becomes a huge problem in middle school. It starts in elementary, but by the time the students hit sixth grade, many have been picked on, teased, and roasted.

We run an activity that helps children see that they are not alone and that teasing hurts everyone. In our ten years of working in this field, we have often seen roasting cross the line and harm others. The problem with roasting and children is they are still trying to understand boundaries, learn appropriate behaviors, and navigate social cues, so when they tease, they quite often don't know when things go too far. This lack of understanding is more pronounced when the students live in an atmosphere of "#Winning" or of being the best; they might try to outdo the last person's roast, to be meaner and more targeted.

Worst of all, roasting can leave some serious emotional scars. Friends know one another's deepest, darkest secrets and use them to make fun of each other. Friends know one another's triggers, fears, and sources of embarrassment. This knowledge is like a rocket filled with ammunition and ready to be launched. When the rocket is launched, it is too late to stop it.

Our solution is to talk about roasting and why it can be painful. Having these conversations earlier, rather than later, can help our children be more empathetic and aware of their words. We go over the different definitions of teasing and talk about the emotions someone might feel when they are teased. We also explore each aspect of teasing and add examples so the children can visualize.

Good Teasing Framework: Good teasing feels good. It is to lighten the mood, add humor, and make the other person feel loved and connected to you. These are examples of good teasing:
- Laughing with someone, not at someone, about something that happened.
- Making a joke in a caring or loving way.
- Knowing someone's temperament and joking in a way that we know they will like.
- Understanding timing and feeling supported in the moment.
- Understanding what is public and private information between each other.
- Being clear about the relationship and teasing in a way that supports the relationship.
- Using the right tone and intention when teasing.

Unintentional Teasing Framework: This type of teasing can enter a gray area. The teasing might include a joke that goes too far, or the timing of the joke might be off. The context could be the problem, or something that used to be funny might become hurtful. The problem might be that sometimes the teaser picks on someone over and over, and even if the teasing is cute, it can get tiring and the person can feel increasingly self-conscious about what is being done or said. Sometimes the teaser's intent is to be funny, but they end up hurting someone. This type of teasing is all about the intention versus the impact. These are examples of unintentional teasing:
- Going too far with a joke, and the teaser's feelings are hurt.
- Intending to be funny but unintentionally sharing too much personal information about a friend.
- Intending to be funny but sharing an embarrassing joke about a friend.
- Intending to make friends laugh, but the joke is hurtful.
- Being too sarcastic.
- Making a mean comment that was meant to be funny.

Mean Teasing Framework: This type of teasing happens when the teaser's intention is to hurt someone. Adults might refer to this type of teasing as jabbing, throwing someone under the bus, or being mean to target someone. It can take the form of a comment, a joke, or sarcasm. It can include repeating something over and over or sharing private information with the intent to embarrass someone. These are examples of mean teasing:
- Intending to harm and not really caring about the impact on others.

- Sharing information to embarrass someone else or to make the teaser look good.
- Name-calling and targeting someone for being different.

Roasting is an intermediate step between unintentional and mean teasing. We should talk about boundaries and explore teasing so that children can better understand this type of teasing.

We use another strategy to fuel connection and kindness in our groups. It is called "positive roasting." Everyone sits in a circle, and when the facilitator or teacher names a particular child, people call out strengths, qualities, and feel-good statements about this child. This exercise creates positive energy, and students try their hardest to outdo themselves. We love using this strategy, and our students gain more insight about what to say to better connect and be kind.

Chapter 16: Friendship Drama

Middle School Letter, 6th Grade: Friendship and Exclusion

Dear Bully,

I know you think I don't like you and I don't miss you. But I always look back to when we used to spend time together and play. When school started you just stopped talking to me, and when me and my friend invited you to go out with us you were just rude and mean to us. You teased my friend about her forehead and said that I hit you with a branch. You said that I was mean to you. I never hit you or did anything to hurt you. I really want to hang out with you again, but I won't until you apologize.

An Old Friend

Dear Victim,

Why did you leave me? School started and you had all these new friends from summer camp. I felt overwhelmed and left out. Like I was so easily replaceable. We have been best friends since first grade.

You went to camp and came back as a different person with all these new friends. It is like I never existed. I felt alone and left out. It was like we were never even best friends. You have all these inside jokes with your new friends and every time I come up to you, I feel like I am just in the way.

How have all these years of friendships been thrown away over one summer? You changed so much, and you were not there for me when I needed you. I am so angry. I don't want to apologize, you are making it all about you. You are selfish and self-involved. So go with your other friends. That is the way things will be from now on. Leave me alone...

The Bully

Middle School Letter, 7th Grade: Friendship Musical Chairs

Dear Bully,

We have this love hate relationship and it causes me a lot of stress. I love to hang out with you, but then you don't let me hang out with other friends. If I play with someone else, you stop talking to me and start hanging out with other girls. I can't win and I am exhausted. I get excited when you are absent, I feel like I can breathe. You are pretty and fun. I love to hang out with you, but I feel like I have to choose between you and my other friends. My mom wants to separate us. She says it is not healthy. I don't know what to think. She says we are fake friends. It hurts me to think that we are fake.

Fake Friend

Dear Victim,

You don't have to hang out with me. You can hang with your other friends. I don't care, like I would care if you didn't hang out with me. You are flattering yourself. I don't need you. I have Ashley and she won't leave me... Ever. You are so fake anyway. Like I need someone like you. Get over yourself.

The Bully

Update: A few weeks later, the second student wrote a new response. This is what she said:

Dear Fake Friend,

It has been a few weeks since we last hung out together and I really miss you. I am sorry to have blown up at you. You are my best friend and I was afraid to lose you. I get so angry and confused when I see you I just snap. I don't mean to bully you. I don't know why I do it.

My older sister is constantly picking on me telling me I am a scaredy cat, my hair is ugly, and that I don't have any friends. She is mean and my mom is so busy with the new baby, I feel alone. I don't mean to hurt you, I am afraid to lose you. So when I get afraid I get mean. I am learning it is my coping mechanism and it is not healthy. I am pushing you away when all I really want is to tell you everything. I want us to spend hours in your room where we laugh and play. We can talk for hours. You never judge me, you are always so nice to me.

Your room is my safe place, I feel like I can be myself. I think I hurt you because I don't know why you are nice to me. How can you be so nice when I am so mean to you?

I don't think your hair is ugly at all. I think it is cool. You don't ever have to brush it cause its so curly. I tell you that cause that is what my sister says to me to control me. I guess I am doing the same. I am sorry for hurting you. I miss you.

Love,

Your BFF (I am done with the bullying)

Stop and Think

Conflict Resolution Between Friends

Friends naturally grow apart, especially in middle school, because they change schools, classrooms, or interests. Friends also use each other to fight the pain they feel. Middle schools breed so many new emotions and interactions that children often cannot process everything that happens in one day. Between the drama of friends, expectations, having to change classrooms, academics, sports, and after-school activities, students sometimes don't know how to resolve conflict. They have sometimes exchanged words, and they don't know how to take them back or make the situation better. We have seen, more times than necessary, good friendships end over simple arguments or because of a lack of resolution. Walking away is sometimes easier, but it is not necessarily better for our emotional well-being.

When dealing with darker, more negative emotions, children often use the people they love the most as punching bags. As adults, we have all done this as well. After a bad day at work, we might come home stressed, angry, irritated, and distracted. We walk into a messy home; dinner is not ready; the house is chaotic, and we lose it. We might yell, say mean things to our children or spouse, or we snap and all hell breaks loose. The daily stress that we encounter can evoke real nasty emotions that can easily be misdirected to the people we love, especially if we are hurt or feel excluded. These emotional outbursts happen; we are all human. But the outbursts never feel good; we feel horrible for what we have said or done.

This kind of emotional misdirection can be difficult for your child to understand. Transitions, bad days, disruptions in their routines, and even small changes cause big reactions. Changes of any kind can invoke anxiety, and sometimes children project their fear, anger, or rejection onto their friends or families.

The letters above demonstrate reactions we see quite often in middle school. These reactions can be overt or more subdued. Adults have experienced these emotions more often and have the tools to cope with change, bad days, and transitions. Middle school children are still learning and trying different coping strategies.

At Bulldog, we address all of the above issues. We explore conflict between friends and try to discover the root cause of arguments. We also talk about apologizing and about learning to forgive one other. We teach children to express themselves, instead of taking their feelings out on the people they love. We help them talk about exclusion and stress, so they don't use their friends or family members as punching bags.

The best thing is to talk about arguments or conflict and help come up with healthy strategies to cope with them. We can talk about why our child is being mean to their friends. Perhaps the meanness is because of another boy or a girl, exclusion, older sibling rivalry, or a change in the home. We can talk about exclusion and the pain of being left out, about the fear of losing a good friend, and about the importance of sharing feelings and resolving conflict instead of shutting down.

We reassure children that we all have weak moments of rage and anger, and we might say mean things. We talk about how our words wound and discuss healthy ways to manage stress and negative emotions. We talk about times we have lost our cool and said something mean. We describe how we felt, the regret we experienced, and how those feelings might have changed some of our relationships. We talk about the importance of apologies and working on being a good friend. For conflict and arguments between friends, we teach students how to resolve conflict. In middle school, they still struggle with reconciling friendships and letting go of the pain of being hurt by their friends.

We have watched children turn into emotional monsters and say mean things that would hurt anyone. We have run parent trainings where parents label their kids as scary, vicious beings. We stop and pause in those moments, take a deep breath and share the following:

A child is not born to hate, to bully, to be mean. Sadly, this behavior is learned from their environment.

It is hard to read that sentence, and often we get a lot of resistance to that idea, but if we dig deeper, we can recall some of the mean stuff we have said to our partners in passing, the fights we have had in front of our children, or the mean gossip or judgments we have passed about our own family or friends. Children are like sponges; they take it all in—the good, the bad, and the nasty. We also tend to be busier than ever, and children are hooked to their tablets, watching unmonitored YouTube shows. They might watch conflict or toxic relationships that play out on screen, or they might see things that they pick up and repeat. We must pay attention to what is being said, done, and watched in our homes.

Friendship Drama

Another middle school challenge is the friendship musical chair syndrome. Middle schoolers go through a phase when exclusion and friends shift. This shift is hard to watch and causes some epic drama within this peer group. One day, a child is at the top of the friendship food chain, and the next day, they are not even on anyone's radar. It is normal for children to want to explore new friendships, but the way this exploration is done can be painful. If a friendship is meant to be, everything will work out, with good coping strategies. We work on being friendly and moving past these friendship transitions with grace, although this work takes some time and patience. During these transitions, we talk about the emotions that come with changes in friendship. The array of emotions might include anger, confusion, rejection, exclusion, jealousy, resentment, rage, revenge, and sadness. Working through each emotion with kind and compassionate conversations can help a child safely navigate these social dynamics.

Below are some questions to explore and adapt to help children work past the friendship musical chairs:

1. When Aiden excludes you at recess, how does that make you feel? Tell me what you are thinking and what you might do. What do you think he is thinking? What would you like to see happen differently? What can you do in that moment to shift from feeling _____ (insert emotion) to a better place? Who else can you play with? What could you do instead of_____ (insert behavior)? Have you ever excluded someone? What drove you to do it? Why does exclusion hurt? What will you do the next time you see exclusion?

2. When Harper tells you that you can't play with her friends, how do you feel? What do you think, and how do you react? When you feel _____ (insert emotion), what do you want to do? What are some things you can do to stop feeling_____ (insert emotion)? Who else can you go hang out with? What can you say to Harper? What do you want to see happen differently?

3. When Emily runs away from you, laughing, how do you feel? _____ (insert emotion) is yucky and is painful. What can you do to have a better recess?

4. When Elijah makes jokes that hurt your feelings, how does it feel? _____ (insert emotion) is not a good feeling. I'm sorry that you have to go through this. What do you want to do to feel better? What do you need to do to have a better recess and stay away from his painful jokes?

5. When Charlotte has inside jokes and doesn't share with you, how do you feel? _____ (insert emotion) is painful. What can you do to not feel left out during recess?

We recommend a three-step process for this work:

I. Identify the behavior, emotions, and thoughts that are painful.
II. Rephrase the feelings and talk them out. Let the children vent, to get all the nasty stories out of their heads.
III. Pivot to a solution or a better feeling for the time being. Getting the child to visualize the situations and play them out gives them the tools and coping strategies to pivot in difficult moments. Troubling interactions only last minutes but can feel like

forever. We want children to realize that they can pivot so that painful interactions that last a few moments don't consume their entire day.

This process takes practice, but the benefits are so rewarding. We can teach our children to problem-solve, visualize, manage emotions, and stand up for themselves.

Conflict Resolution Techniques

If children desire to work on the friendship, we recommend talking to the other parents and finding options for resolution. We can suggest setting up a time when the adults can meet—perhaps on the weekend and in a safe zone. We can use a neutral mediator or have a parent on each side help with communication.

Parents who do this mediation process should keep their opinions, parental recommendations, or judgments checked at the door. They might get triggered and want to save their children, but they would be doing no good in the situation.

The following are some guidelines for the mediation, as parents or their children talk out the issues:

1. Use "I" statements versus "you" statements. Take the blame out of the conversation.
2. Stay away from "but" and replace it with "and."
3. Avoid name-calling or bringing up other people in the discussion. Talk about only the people at the table.
4. Remember that the goal for this conversation is to come to a resolution that works for both parties.
5. End with an apology from both sides.
6. Work on sharing what the children loved about their friendship or what they love about each other.

Examples of the guidelines in action:

1. "I'm hurt that I was excluded from the group. I felt left out at recess."
   > instead of "You hurt me when you excluded me from the group. You left me out at recess." Using "I" statements instead of "you" statements creates a difference in tone and direction.

2. "I want to work on our friendship, and I need some time."
   > instead of "I want to work on our friendship, but I need some time." The tone becomes negative when we use "but." Keep your "but" out of it. There is no room for "but" in conflict resolution.

3. "When you're with your friends, you talk about me. I heard what you said about me, and it hurt me."
   > instead of "When Mia and Charlotte were with you, Ava told me what you said about me." These many names make it difficult to follow what actually

happened. We must go back to the interaction, not what other people said or thought happened. Naming other people suggests gossip and can fuel more drama. We should stick to the people sitting at the table and their actions. Talking about the intent and impact of their actions is more productive than engaging in a "he said-she said-they said" said cycle.

4. "What do we want from this conversation? How can we resolve this to mend the friendship or walk away with some friendly strategies to better get along?" instead of "We're not leaving here until you two are friends again." Sometimes, in middle school, children need more time to process, forgive, and rebuild their friendships. We should start with baby steps, develop a plan, walk through the plan, and close with an agreement for the next steps.

5. We must work on apologizing. In a genuine apology, we need to admit to our wrong, explain why it hurt (show empathy), talk about the next steps to make amends, and ask for forgiveness. These are the types of statements or questions we can use:
    i. "I'm sorry for_____." (admit behavior)
    ii. "This is wrong, because_____."
    iii. "Starting now, I will _____."
    iv. "Will you forgive me?"

6. We can close the mediation by sharing what the other person appreciates, loves, or misses from the friendship. When each child takes turns, we can see the shift in their emotions. They will feel more content, joyful, and appreciative.

If the friendship cannot be repaired or if it is time for the children to dissolve the friendship, we can get our child involved in a new activity where they have the opportunity to make new friends with others who share the same interests. We can get them involved in different groups and help them learn how to make new friends and find people who have similar interests. Building a network of friends will add so much to a child's emotional bank account.

To conclude, transitions with friends are only one kind of change children experience in middle school. As adults, we underestimate the degree to which transitioning grades, school, and experiences affects our children. We must remember to be allies in these situations. We can teach our kids healthy coping strategies. We can dance it out, sing it out, act it out. We can exercise their brains through visualization. We can help them find the tools that will work for them.

Chapter 17: Toxic Friendships and Exclusion

Middle School Letter, 6th Grade: Frenemies

Dear Bully,

Whenever I'm around you it feels like I can't be myself. You're not necessarily a bully, but you don't make me feel the best. Whenever you make a rude joke that I didn't realize was rude, I would laugh with you. Now I realize it's not funny how you make me feel in school. I can't raise my hand to speak up because you'll criticize me. You give me looks and giggle. I realized that you're two faced. You have a funny caring side sometimes but you do have a mean, evil, and rude side too. I can't stop being "afraid" to speak up because I haven't spoken up since the first time I got roasted. I can't be myself at all. Stop it! I want to speak up.

Afraid to Speak Up

Dear Afraid to Speak Up,

This is a hard situation, as this person seems to be someone who you thought was your friend. Often, in middle school, our bodies change, our interests change, and our friends change. You are in the midst of all of this change. It is hard, and I want you to find your voice. Think about what you would say to your younger sibling or cousin. Would you want them to live in fear of mockery? No, you would like for them to be happy. So why do you let yourself feel this way? Do you want to live in fear of being yourself? That is not fun and really is not healthy.

Relationships with our friends should leave us with good energy, not tear us down. Often, our friends can seem like the biggest, meanest bullies. They know our secrets, they know our weaknesses, and they know how to strike us where it hurts. Toxic friendships creep up on us all the time. Don't get sucked into the drama and toxicity of a bad friendship. Roasting hurts. It is the worst kind of bullying that I have seen.

We all have the right to remove ourselves from any situation that does not fulfill us in a positive way. I want you to start thinking of the friends you want in your circle. It is in our control to choose our friends. You want friends who make you feel good and whom you trust. I recommend that you start finding new activities or new groups of friends. Sign up for an activity or sport you always wanted to try and in which the bully friend does not participate. Find something that you really like to do. In finding new interests, you will meet new people. Stay behind at recess and see if you can help other students or the teacher. Find new after-school activities that you are passionate about or good at and change the pace. Find someone you can talk to about your feelings, someone who really listens to you, someone you trust.

Friendship can be tricky in middle school, but you don't have to fall into a pattern of fear of being yourself. You have choices. You might not see them today, but tomorrow will bring something new.

Your friends don't have control over you. You have control over your emotions and choices. So choose differently! Empower yourself to speak up and try something new.
At first, it will be hard. Change is always hard. Change just one thing tomorrow, and I promise it will all start shifting.

Next time your toxic friend gives you a look or giggle, take your power back and walk away or turn around. Tell yourself you are over this and think about who makes you happy. I know you can take your power back. I believe in you. Don't let this be part of you. Let it be a turning point in middle school, and if the meanness continues, tell a teacher you trust. Don't stop telling until someone listens. You are not alone. I promise this happens so much, and often we don't talk about it out of fear. Be the one to stand up against fear and make a difference. I promise you the best revenge is finding new friends being happy with them. When we find joy, it is so easy for us to let go of the nasty stuff, let go of resentment, let go of toxic friendships. Why, you might ask? Well, you won't have time for the drama. You will be too busy enjoying your own life.

Sending you so much love and positivity,

The Bully Teacher

Middle School Letter, 6th Grade: Exclusion and Rumors

Dear Bully,

You pick on me, you lie, I see you roll your eyes at me whenever I speak and it hurts. I always notice your facial expressions when I speak and honestly, it makes me not want to raise my hand or talk in class. I know that you have started rumors about me and that really hurt because then all my friends has turned on me. I am tired of all of your crap. It is annoying! I just don't get why you act like that!

Tired and Annoyed

Dear Victim,

I wish I could let you into my world. I wish I could stop. I wish that everyone would stop. I am done. I am over this school. I get blamed for everything and then my mom needs to come to school. I am angry all the time. School has blamed me for so many things, most of them I didn't do, so now I lie. I lie to protect myself. I lie to get out of trouble, because if not I got a beating waiting for me. My mom has this new boyfriend and each time the school calls, he takes care of it. I hate him. I hate her. She is starting to compare herself to me. She is acting weird and annoying.

She thinks I am dumb. She lies to me. I know when she is high or drunk. I use to have school to escape but now I have nothing. I know I shouldn't have started those rumors about you, but I know you overheard my mom scream at me, before we entered school. I know you heard her tell me how I am the worst thing that ever happened to her. That my dad is a junky, and that I am a little whore showing off to her new boyfriend. I was ashamed. So I started a rumor before you could gossip about me. I got to protect myself, because if I don't no one will.

I am sorry for what I said about you.

The Bully

Middle School Letter, 6th Grade: Exclusion and Drama

Dear Bully,

Whenever you teased me about stupid things it hurts my feelings and it makes me look bad in front of others. I feel so embarrassed when you do it. You are constantly staring at me, and then you laugh at me when I pass you in the hallways.

I've seen people make fun of you, and I know it hurts your feelings. I feel the same way too, I get hurt the same way. I just want you to stop saying those things. I really want to be your friend! I don't know how to fix this.

Over the Drama

Dear Over the Drama,

In middle school there's often a lot of drama or back-and-forth conflict. It can be exhausting. When it's not addressed or we don't get to its root cause, it can easily start over again, with the same people. It can be so aggravating. It's a "She said-He said-They said" war that can leave teachers and counselors exhausted.

I think it's time to really think about your impact on these interactions:
- What have you done in the past to maybe hurt your old friend?
- Did you exclude her or make fun of her?

I'm not blaming you for the teasing, I'm trying to open up opportunities for a mediation and learn more about the entire story of your friendship.

Sometimes, we might overthink situations. When we think someone is talking about us or looking at us, we often assume that they are. We (the Bully Teachers) call this "target assumption"—when we think everyone is looking at or talking about us. We might make this kind of assumption if we've dealt with trauma, bullying, and constant exclusion, but we're usually more wrong than right. Our brains and bodies want to protect us, so we focus on finding who might be talking about us, instead of finding joy or fun in a situation. If you ever felt like you walked into a room and everyone was talking about you, more often than not, your imagination was playing tricks on you. Your mind would rather protect you and lead you down a false path than have you be the subject of ridicule.

I'd love to see you love yourself a little more and find ways to gain back your power. Below are some ideas I want you to think about:

1. When you think someone is staring at you, say hi and smile.
2. When you think someone is laughing at you, ask what they are laughing at and if you can join in.
3. If they're mean to you, then create some one-liners to help you.
4. When they are alone, you can go up to them and ask them why they laugh at you.
5. If you want to understand the root cause of this drama, you can get the counselor involved and do a mediation.

How would you feel if you no longer feared walking into a room? How would it feel to have the confidence to stand up for yourself or smile at someone who is looking at you? Think about the answers to those questions.

Don't let anyone put the victim badge on you. Shift your thinking to a more positive side, to give yourself some room to breathe. Think about what strategies or ideas you can use to protect yourself. Reclaim your power. Focus on loving yourself and finding ways to get back to joy.

Sending you love and positivity,

The Bully Teacher

Middle School Letter, 7th Grade: Exclusion and Drama

Dear Bulldog,

At Halloween a group of girls were going to do a group costume and they didn't invite me so I was a little upset. They then decided they didn't want to do that costume anymore so they asked if they could do what I was doing with two other people. I said yes because I didn't want to be a hypocrite or hurt their feelings. What got me upset was that they then decided they didn't want to be what we were being so they made a new group and costume and didn't invite me, again. I was very upset, angry and hurt because I was nice to them even though they weren't to me that first time and they still decided to be mean.

Halloween Costume

Dear Halloween Costume,

I am sorry that you were left out and felt hurt. If I were in this situation, I'd feel the same way, like my friends had taken advantage of me. I've talked to students from all different backgrounds, and I've heard multiple versions of this story. However, the emotions and hurt in each version are all the same.

This story gives us a few things to consider.

My first piece of advice is to focus on yourself and consider your own feelings. I urge you to find a group of friends that will stay with you through all seasons—not just the ones who are friendly when it benefits them or is convenient to them. It was nice of you to allow your friends to use your costume idea when they asked; however, do you think they would have done the same for you? You said that you didn't want them to feel bad, but I encourage you to remember your own feelings in that moment, too.

My second piece of advice is going to make you the bigger and better person. Remember to include others and make them feel as if they aren't outsiders. Recall your feeling of being left out, and don't let others feel the same way. I've asked many students this question: "How can you be inclusive?" Some students have said that when they witness someone being excluded from a group, they invite them to join their group, or when a new student comes, they introduce themselves and sit with them at lunch. Sometimes all we need is a friend or for someone to listen to us. We can take the hurt from our own experience and use it to keep others from feeling that pain.

If we're kind to one another, that kindness can plant the seed for others to be kind. Although your friends didn't invite you and you were hurt, you can now use this experience to help others and to remember the importance of including others.

The Bully Teacher

Middle School Letter, 7th Grade: Social Acceptance

Dear Bulldog,

I went to school and no one talked to me. This happened for a whole week. The next week, I heard from someone that they were shunning me because I didn't like everything they liked. They stopped and I guess they felt guilty because they don't like bullying. I am so confused. I get excluded for not being like everyone else. Now they feel guilty but no one is talking to me.

Alone and Confused.

Dear Alone and Confused,

Exclusion hurts. You feel as though you're the only one; you're disconnected from everyone. It's like there's a huge party, and you never got invited. It sucks, and I'm sorry. One week, you have friends, and the next, no one talks to you. You're constantly on eggshells, trying to figure out the right thing to do and say.

Remember that you're not alone. Every middle school student feels this way. I've been doing this work for a very long time, and middle school is tough. I say, "Survive middle school, and you win at life!" It's a constant battle of peer pressure, parental pressure, exposure to new things, and risk-taking behaviors. You might be rolling your eyes, but it's true. You're learning to navigate complicated emotions and situations, but you're not alone.

Be yourself; you'll find friends who like the stuff that you like. Talk to new people, or when someone ignores you, walk away and find someone new. Don't play the nasty game of exclusion; it's exhausting. Be yourself and focus on you. If you like gaming, talk about it and find friends who play the same games. We've been at your school for a while; we know that there are many kids you don't know really well, and you could develop new friendships. Don't get caught up in the group you feel you should hang out with because you've been friends since kindergarten. Move on to new friends and interests.

Your question about whether you'll get excluded today exudes so much stress and anxiety. Focus on what you love, and friends will come to you. Be the one who doesn't care about inclusion, and you'll see things start to change. It takes one kid to change the cycle. It takes one kid to take a stand, and you'll see that people will be drawn to you. I see you, and I know you have it in you to move away from all this exclusion. It's stressful, and you don't need that. Find what you love and do it more. Doing what you love will bring you joy and a whole lot of new friends who won't exclude you.

Sending you lots of love and gratitude,

The Bully Teacher

Middle School Letter, 8th Grade: Friendship and Posting on Social Media

Dear Bully,

I know that we are close friends and we have been for awhile but there are some thing's that only I can say about myself. For example, when I said I'm not photogenic you were like "no, no you are not...Whatever!!!" and you roll your eyes and laugh at me. You do things like that a lot. It makes me feel bad about myself and I don't like it. I tell you all the time that I think I am ugly, fat, and a loser. I feel like you mock my insecurities and you use the pictures to make yourself look good. I don't like selfies. I don't feel pretty and you making me take pictures and laughing at me only hurts me more. I hate that you share our pictures on Snapchat or Instagram. In some of them I look awful and you make it worse by commenting and sharing. I wish you would stop.

The Unselfie Friend

Dear Unselfie Friend,

We want to go back and talk about a few things. First, this is your best friend, and you need to talk to her about these issues. If you feel like she's purposely posting bad pictures of you, then I'd recommend that you reconsider this friendship. Your best friend should make you feel safe and supported. You also have the power to ask her to take the pictures down. You have a right to your privacy. She needs your permission to post a photo of you. She can actually get into trouble if she does post pictures without your permission. If I were you, I'd talk to her about the situation and explain how all of this makes you feel. If things don't change within a week, and this is still going on, then I'd suggest taking a break from her and reminding her that until she changes her selfie ways, you don't want to hang out anymore. We forget that we can break up with friends, too. We don't have to stay in toxic friendships. Talk to her, and if things don't change, break up!

Second, remember that you're beautiful. Own your beauty, and don't put yourself down. We live in a world that constantly judges or criticizes us. You don't need to do that to yourself. Stare at yourself in the mirror for at least sixty seconds and repeat, "I am beautiful. I am pretty. I am unique. I am strong. I am…" Fill in the blanks. Say, "I love me. I am worthy. I am enough." If you feel weird, then try using the second person: "I love you. You are worthy. You are enough." You have to use positive words. You might cry at first. This exercise can be emotional, but keep doing it. You don't even need to use "I am" or "You are" statements. You can list the features you like about yourself: "I like my hair, my eyes, my skin, my hands, my feet, my mouth, my laugh, my smile…" Keep going; find things that you like about yourself and build a list. Don't focus on what you don't like; focus on what you do like. This simple exercise can boost your self-esteem and self-worth. You have to do it. Eventually, you'll pass a mirror and say, "I look good" or "Hello, gorgeous."

You want to build momentum with positive words firing from your brain. This is the only way you'll start to feel pretty. Believe me. I've been through it and seen so many teens try to change everything about themselves. Even when they've changed everything, they still feel "unpretty." So find what you like about yourself, and learn to love it.

The mirror activity is a must-do!

Sending you love and positivity,

The Bully Teacher

Stop and Think

Toxic Versus Healthy Friendships

Often, children do not know the difference between a toxic and a healthy friendship. We have concluded that a lot of parents are still trying to figure out the difference, as they meet and get to know each other.

A toxic friendship is an unsafe or untrusting relationship that feels unsupported or fake. It can be a relationship with someone who always takes advantage of others. They are not considerate of other people's emotions. They use the friendship as a weapon. They can be selfish, dishonest, manipulative, controlling, exclusive, and overbearing. They can make friends feel really special if they do what they want, but when friends don't listen, they turn on them or mock them. They say hurtful things to their friends, to make them feel bad. They use information as a currency and turn people against each other. They might be judgmental or really negative. They constantly seek favors from friends and never return the favors. They gossip and spread rumors to protect themselves. They twist stories to make themselves look good or needed. When we're around them, we're cautious and fearful. We don't feel like ourselves and often have to prove ourselves to feel some sort of worth.

A healthy friendship is a safe or trusting relationship that feels supported and filled with love. In it, we can be our true authentic selves. It is a place where our secrets are in a vault, and we can feel at home. A healthy friendship shows trustworthiness, loyalty, dependability, and a mutual respect for one another. It is a place where we feel safe saying we're sorry, and we know we can be forgiven. It is a place where we can talk about anything without judgment.

We can discuss the characteristics of toxic friendships with our children, in order for them to recognize whether they are in these types of relationship. Toxic friendships have the following characteristics:

1. We constantly give and do things for the other person—like favors, homework, or helping them out.
2. The other person does not help or ask how they can help. They assume helping is not their responsibility.
3. They never ask us how we are feeling or let us talk about our feelings, unless those feelings are about them.
4. We doubt ourselves or feel self-conscious around them. We question everything. We become unsure of ourselves.
5. We apologize for their behavior towards others. We see that they hurt others, and we apologize for their wrongdoing.
6. We do not feel good about who we are when we are with them. We feel like we are being fake or imitating our friend, and it does not feel good.
7. We feel peer pressure to engage in their risky behaviors.
8. We feel like we are in constant competition with them. We are never good enough.

9. We fear being ridiculed or excluded if we don't follow their lead.
10. We put up with them mocking us and putting us down.

When we're in a healthy relationship, we cheer each other on and feel safe within each other's company.

As parents, if we fear that our child has a toxic friend, we should first make sure that the friend really is toxic and then work with our child to end or take a time out from the friendship. Having conversations with our children and paying attention to their friends in middle school is critical. We can ask a lot of open-ended questions and learn about our child's interests. We should be curious about who they select as their friends and why. We can ask them what is important to them in a friendship and about the different type of friends they have. However, as parents, we sometimes fail to see the whole picture, and we might be too quick to intervene. We should stay away from shaming or being too authoritative when it comes to our children's social circles.

Our children might have the following friendships:
- Best friends
- Neighborhood friends
- School friends
- Family friends
- Camp friends
- Sports team friends
- Church friends
- After-school friends
- Fun friends
- Gaming friends
- Online friends
- Chat friends

The list can go on and on. We should ask our children about their different friend groups, what their different friendships are like, and what they value from them. The ideal situation is for a child to have different groups of friends, so if one friendship turns sour, then they can turn to another group of friends, helping them process the loss and giving them an out if they are dealing with peer pressure. Our children should develop a network of friends or people with whom they are friendly, to keep their social circles open. Friendships in middle school are constantly evolving, and this change can be exhausting for our children. When they have other groups of friends that might be more stable, children will feel more stable, more resilient, and more eager to let go of a toxic relationship.

We use some strategies and suggestions to help children step away from a toxic friendship and reflect on what they want for themselves. Parents and teachers must make time for these conversations and be honest. They should be present and not dismiss any emotions. It is a hard thing for anyone to break up with a friend. We want to be supportive and open to our children's decisions.

We should read the text below and walk through it with our children:

Taking a timeout from your friend might be the solution you need. If you truly recognize that someone is no good for you, it might be better to step away and take a break from the other person. But of course, this is a lot easier said than done. Breaking up with a friend is hard to do. It takes some strength and resilience. We recommend you end the friendship in a way that you feel safe. You might do it over the phone or face-to-face. Avoid texting, as it is easy to copy and paste the content and share it. Sometimes that can backfire. Make sure you are in a neutral zone, and you don't end up attacking or feeling attacked. Use "I" statements versus "You" statements, and watch out to not blame the other person as you explain the friendship break.

Friendship Break-up Narrative

Below are some sample breakup narratives:

"Hey, Molly, I'm sorry I haven't been hanging around. I got really busy. After taking some time away from hanging out with you, I realized that we might need to take a break in our friendship. I loved hanging out with you, but lately, I don't feel good about myself when we hang out. We fight or compete with each other, and that doesn't make me feel good. It's not you. We're growing apart and finding new friends. I'll always keep your secrets and be there for you, but we just need a little space. You've been playing more with Charlotte and Emma. I've been hanging out with Sophie and Talia. Our friends are shifting, and maybe we can hang out with new people for a little while. I care so much for you that I want us both to be happy and not compete."

"Hey, Helen, we've been fighting a lot lately. Our last fight got out of control. I accept my responsibility. I'm sorry I called you names, yelled at you, and tried to hurt you. I did it because you hurt me, too. It's not okay that I behaved that way. I'm sorry I hurt you. I'm hurting, too. Going through that epic fight and turning our friends against each other was wrong. I don't want to be that person. I want us to take a break from being friends. I don't want to be enemies. I want what's best for each of us. It's going to be hard, but we need to both heal and find healthy friendships that don't start so much drama. I want us to be mature and friendly. So that means no talking behind each other's backs, no eye rolls or stink eyes. That means saying hi to each other in passing. I think it would be good for both of us to take some time and think about what we want with this friendship. What do you think? How can I best support what you need?"

"Hey, Isabella, I've really loved hanging out with you, until lately. We're not getting along, and when I hang out with you, I don't feel good about myself. I question my choices, I'm negative, and I'm very judgmental. I think we need a break so I can work on myself to feel good about who I am."

"Hey, Bobby, you're a great friend to me, but I don't like how you treat others. That's not okay with me. I want to take a time out from hanging out with you. You need to figure out why you're being so mean. I don't want to get involved anymore."

"Hey, Madison, I don't like how we talk to each other. It hurts my feelings when you mock me and make fun of me. I don't want to feel like this anymore. I want to take a break from being friends. I think we're both on different paths."

"Hey, Logan, we've been friends since kindergarten, and I think we're ready to take a break and explore new friendships. We have different interests, and you're so important to me. I don't want us to fight or turn on each other because we feel left out. We can check in with each other, but I want us to hang out with new friends, so we can expand our circle. I'll always be here for you. I just want us to have space to meet new people."

We can take any of these samples above and tailor them to fit our child's style of communication. The important point is to be clear about what they want and that they take responsibility for their actions, stay away from blame or judgment, and are kind. Breakup and timeout are hard, so they should do them with kindness, staying away from attitude or anger, which will only fuel retaliation.

When children end a toxic relationship, there can be some repercussions that we should explore with them. We can talk about the following and come up with strategies:

Retaliation: When the friend wants to seek revenge because the child doesn't want to be friends with them anymore, we can help the child come up with answers to the following questions:
- What will you do if they turn on you?
- How will it feel?
- What can you do to feel safe and not sucked into the drama?
- What will you do if you hear rumors or gossip about you because of the breakup?
- What are five positive coping strategies to help you address any retaliation threats?

Regret or Fear of Missing Out (FOMO): A child might feel bad about breaking up with a friend or feel like things will change if they give the friendship another chance. They might second-guess themselves or dismiss some of the pain they felt during the friendship. They might even tell themselves that the friendship was really not that bad. In those moments, we can show them that their feeling of regret indicates a good time to step away from and examine the situation. Distraction a great strategy for when children feel regret. We can find activities with our children to keep them distracted, off of social media, and away from spending too much time regretting their decision. We can help them come up with answers to the following questions:

- What will you do when you see all your old friends hanging out on Snapchat?
- How will you feel, and what do you want to do differently?
- What are some things that can distract you from FOMO or regret?
- Who are some friends who make you feel safe, supported, and good about yourself?

Friendship drama is a big part of middle school. It can impact a classroom, grades, and a child's self-esteem. It is important to talk about healthy friendships, to have examples of good versus bad friends, and to determine the type of friends a child needs in their life. The following are ideas to use to start those conversations:

- When watching a movie or TV show together, talk about the good and bad friendships in the program.
- When discussing a book, talk about the characters and identify healthy versus unhealthy relationships.
- When listening to music, ask about the musicians and their friendship or support system.
- When watching sports, discuss teamwork and healthy relationships and friendship.
- When having dinner or riding in the car, talk about different friendships and ask questions to gain more insight.
- Share stories of toxic versus healthy friendship but avoid talking about other parents at the school, as that will only fuel drama.

Chapter 18: Toxic Romantic Relationships

High School Letter, 9th Grade: Toxic Romantic Relationship

Dear Bully,

You made me feel stupid for opening up my heart and showing my emotions to you when we were dating. I trusted you to understand me and how I felt but now I feel as if I closed off the world after you broke my heart. It hurts to know that I went to great lengths to make you happy but you took advantage of me. You never let me be me and always wanted me to act a certain way. I never was able to be me or talk to you about how I felt about things. But like you said, "I'm a man" so I should be able to control these emotions and not show them.

Not Man Enough

Dear Not Man Enough,

I am sorry that you feel as if you can't or shouldn't show your emotions. As humans, we're emotional creatures, and whether you're a man or not, you should be able to show your emotions and talk about how you feel. It hurts to go through a rough breakup. You feel as if you want to close off the world, but please don't. The world is a wonderful place, filled with wonderful people. You may go through tough breakups, but you can take a step back and see what you've learned, in order not to make the same mistakes again. Taking a step back can also help you talk about what is a healthy relationship and what is not. If the person you're dating is hurting you, or not allowing you to be yourself, most likely that relationship is toxic.

These are a few ways to tell if you're in an unhealthy relationship:

1. You constantly try to please your partner, but they don't do the same for you. You give your all while they don't do the same for you. There is an imbalance in the relationship, and if there is no balance, the relationship can be toxic.

2. You feel unsure within yourself and about yourself. In order to please your partner, you start to question things about yourself—the way you look, the way you dress, how you talk, what you say, and what you like.

3. Your partner drains your energy with hurtful comments that take away from your self-confidence.

These are some things to look for and to be aware of when in a relationship. If you're feeling any of these, it's time to leave the relationship.

Remember to always be yourself and love yourself. You are your most important relationship.

Sending you Love and Positivity,

The Bully Teacher

High School Letter, 10th Grade: Toxic Romantic Relationship

Dear Bully,

You're manipulative, toxic, abusive, and I know you haven't changed. I don't know how I ever loved you and cared for you as if you were family. You treated me like crap. You put me down. Even now, after a year of not talking, you still have to come after me. You took away one of the things that I wanted to do most, what would've helped me out of this huge depressing hole I was stuck in. You have everyone on your side because you cry and label yourself a victim. One of these days, all your lies will unfold, and everything will be revealed. You're in "misery" and now, without you, I'm happy. Happier without you in my life. All you were was a brick dragging me down and using me to put yourself in a higher place. Well, guess what? You would've never gotten that high without me.

Finally Free

Dear Finally Free,

It sounds like you were in a very toxic relationship. We're proud of you for recognizing your worth and removing yourself from the situation. As we become older, we sometimes realize that no matter how pure our intentions are, we cannot change certain people. However, we can change and control ourselves, and that's important to remember. We're responsible for removing ourselves from situations that do not make us feel respected, safe, or appreciated. We should never feel emotionally drained in every encounter with an individual. It takes a lot of self-realization to walk away from a situation like you did.

Right now, maintenance is important. Remember your worth. Recognize that if someone claims that they have changed, there should be continuous behaviors that back up that claim, not just words. Remember the way you felt when you were with that person—unsettled, unfulfilled, and not appreciated. Then, remember the way you feel when you're not with that person—independent, strong, and happy. Your happiness stands alone and is not dependent on someone else's actions.

We're proud of you for being strong and taking the correct steps. Stay strong to see it through. Surround yourself with people who love you, see your worth, and don't drag you down.

Sending you Love and Positivity,

The Bully Teacher

Stop and Think

High School Romantic Relationships

When students enter high school, they naturally want to have relationships. Sometimes, the pressure is so great for them that they enter relationships that are not true fits. The pressure can come from a desire to fit in, the fact that a crush is finally paying attention to them, or the fact that the "bad boy" is so cool and hot. The list goes on, but these are the wrong reasons to get involved with someone who will harm someone and take their self-worth.

As Bully Teachers, we have seen our fair share of "bad boys" or "wild ones." As teens, we have also had our fair share of bad-boy encounters. Bad boys seem so mysterious, so dark, so worthwhile. If they date us, we know we can get through to them. We can change them. More often than not, we end up brokenhearted and hooked on the one that got away.

Now that we have worked with some of these "bad boys," we have learned that, whether one of these children is labeled a "bad boy" or a "wild child," they are not bad to the bone, they are not broken, and it is not up to us to fix them. These boys are in a lot of pain, have issues trusting others, are sad, and usually need help. We would love to think that a romantic relationship would sweep them off their feet, but more often than not, it can drag the other person through the wringer, into the territory of a toxic relationship.

Children want to feel connected, accepted, loved, and appreciated. Sometimes, they look for these things all in the wrong places. Having honest conversations about partnership and dating is important. Discussing self-respect and mutual pleasure is also important. At Bulldog, we have countless discussions about sex and mutual consent. We are not sex educators, but we try our best to explain the importance of love and respect, as well as the desire that burns in the hearts of children. Having frequent chats earlier in middle school can open up the door to trust and communication when it comes to dating and sex.

We encountered one mother who started talking to her children about mutual consent and sex when they were very young. She explained that sex is more than intercourse and that oral sex is still sex. She did not shun her children and, instead, opened the door to questions about sexuality. Now, all of her children's friends turn to her for advice and guidance. She has become the support the group needed to have difficult conversations and to navigate relationships.

Another mother was a nurse and did something we think is quite brilliant. She found out about her children's sex-ed class in middle school (8th grade) and that night, printed out pictures of STDs and what happens to someone's body when they have contracted such a disease. Her children were all boys. She left them the pictures, some condoms, and wrote them a note that said, "If you chose to have sex, use a rubber, because this is what I see at work." The boys went on to high school and college without ever forgetting protection.

As parents, we each have our own way of communicating. When discussing relationships and sexuality with our children, we just need to find comfort in being uncomfortable. By avoiding the subject, we put our children at risk for unaffectionate, one-sided relationships or toxic, harmful relationships. These topics need to be addressed, as we see so much slut-shaming and bullying around sexual activity.

To clarify, toxic relationships are any relationships that significantly take away from one or both of the individuals involved. They can take away someone's freedom, their self-esteem, their self-worth, their happiness, and more. In healthy relationships, there is no pressure to do anything that someone does not want to do. Toxic relationships are fueled by jealousy, physical and verbal abuse, and insecurities. Toxic relationships can be romantic or platonic.

Toxic relationships can sometimes be difficult to identify, and they can develop over time. When relationships go on for a long time and there is much time invested in them, the individuals in the relationship might refuse to see that it is time to cut the cord and move on.

For a teenager, dating for a month can seem like forever. Being with a partner for over six months can make a relationship seem like it has always been. Teenagers often believe that their partners will never leave them. We return to the FAN syndrome, and we can chat about healthy choices and how nothing is forever or always or never.

For parents or adults who care, it can be difficult to tell if the teenager (or anyone) in their lives is involved in a toxic relationship. Some of the signs of a toxic relationship are a loss of self-identity, low self-esteem/ self-confidence, and a loss of interest.

We once spoke to a young lady about the high school legacy that the members of her class would leave behind after they left high school. When we asked how she would be known, she said that people would remember her "for being Marty's girlfriend." This broke our hearts. She had attached all of her identity to her partner.

Before a relationship starts, it is important to remember that we are all individuals, and healthy relationships are meant to make us better "persons" than we were before. Toxic relationships tend to be more unstable than healthy relationships. There can be more break-ups, fights, or drama, and they are fueled by big emotions. One day, a couple can seem very happy and obsessed with one other. On other days, they can seem very upset, erratic, and consumed by the relationship. If we see something like this happening to our teenager, we should remind them that we have never seen a long-term relationship "make it" when it was on-again, off-again.

If we notice that our child is losing interest in things they once liked, we should consider talking to them about their relationship and about what they value in the relationship. This discussion should be a continuous conversation. We can reinforce our child's values, their strengths, and what brings them joy. Once we can connect to their true desires in a relationship, we can help them become aware of the self-destruction in their current relationship. We should be careful not to blame or point out the toxicity we see, as we can create resistance and our child might shut down. It is important to create a safe place where they feel that they can openly share their thoughts about their relationship. As teachers and as parents, our involvement throughout the relationship will be one of the best indicators of if or when the relationship turns toxic. We can tell our teenagers that we are always there for them and just want them to be happy, to be safe, and to feel respected. We can find examples to share about healthy and unhealthy relationships so they can relate to them. The support and knowledge that we give them will help them make healthy decisions when it comes to relationships.

Chapter 19: Self-Esteem Thermometer

Middle School Letter, 8th Grade: Body Shaming and Self-Esteem

Dear Bully,

You always make fun of my body and say that I am too skinny. You talk about me when we change at gym. You make fun of me because I don't have boobs and you tell everyone that I am a flat chested freak! I am afraid to change in the locker room. I just sit there and take it. I am so furious at myself. You get all the boys attention, you hit puberty in 6th grade. You wear makeup and have all the friends. You get invited to the cool parties and hang out with teens. Why even bother to pick on me. You know what I would do to look like you? You have no idea how hard it is to not be like all the other girls in 8th grade. To be small and skinny. To be told I am so cute and pat me on the head. I am sick of all of it. I am sick of you.

I just deal with your crap until I get home. I lock myself in my room and cry until dinner. Often I force feed myself, but I am sick to my stomach thinking about how you gain pleasure over ridiculing my body. Slamming me for being skinny. I hate my body, I hate myself, I hate middle school, I hate you!

The Skinny Girl

Dear Victim,

I apologize for making fun of your body calling you "Skinny Bitch", "Flat as a pancake, stiff as a board." I point at you and laugh, I pass by you and make fun of your padded bra. I feel bad because I see how it hurts you, but when I am around you I get so angry, like I feel I am going to explode...

I am really jealous and I deny it, but all I want to be is skinny. I want to look like you. I have these big boobs that hurt my back, and I can gain control of my weight. I have to wear all this makeup because my skins constantly breaking out. You are so thin with glowing skin, you look beautiful. Sports come so easy to you. I watch you during our drills and you are so fast and strong. I get so annoyed because I don't have any upper body strength. I sometimes think about what it is like to be you. I imagine your mom being so kind and loving. Asking about your day and being so excited to be with you. I am sure your mom is nothing like mine.

My mom puts me on these crazy diets and makes me watch everything I eat. One week it is Keto, the other is Paleo, or low carb. She hides sugar and treats from me. When we go out to eat, she will make remarks or give me a look if I order a Coke instead of Diet Coke. She says to me: "A minute on your lips and forever on your hips." "No one likes a fat girl."

She calls me chubby, big bone, and reminds me that fat girls are losers. She then says: "Do you want to be a loser?" She is constantly criticizing me and making comments on my size. The other day, she said that when she was in high school she was prettiest and most popular girl. She said that it was too bad I was fat, I would never fit in her cool vintage clothes. She said the only reason I am popular is because I went through puberty in 5th grade. She is always working out and making me an example of how lazy people get fat.

I hide snacks and cookies in my room. I eat my emotions. I will never be skinny enough or pretty enough for my mom. She has never told me I was beautiful. She buys me clothes either too small or too big. I tell her my size and she still does that to me. It is like this painful game to go shopping with her. People think she is the coolest, she loves to show off, but behind clothes doors, she is mean and spiteful. I am in pain, I cut myself, and I hate my body. When I see you, I am filled with rage. You are so thin and light. I just want to be you. I think if I was more like you, my mom would love me. I am sorry to have hurt you. I am hurting so bad. I am fat and alone.

The Bully

Middle School Letter, 7th Grade: Body Shaming and Self-Bullying

Dear Bully,

You are such a loser. You are ugly, fat, and invisible. No one cares about you. You should drink bleach and die. You keep hurting yourself and people don't even care...

I'm sorry for all the times I've hurt myself. I'm sorry for the way I am. I am sorry I hate myself.

My Unlovable Self

Dear Unlovable Self,

This is what your older self wants to say to you: "I want us to have a heart-to-heart today. I see the way you treat yourself. You scar your body. I am here to tell you that it gets so much better after middle school.

You won't believe it, but you are in love. You are top of your class, and you are happy. You are really happy. Your parents finally divorced, and you go to family therapy. Your mom opened up to you, and you got a dog. Start spending more time journaling and less time on social media. Social media is a time-sucker! Stop comparing yourself to others, and start looking at what makes you special. Learn to love yourself, and all of a sudden, things will shift. It is pretty cool. I am telling you all this, because you don't have to hurt yourself. You have to start believing in yourself.

Stop putting yourself down because you think you are worthless. Your parents' divorce is not your fault! Turn to your friends for help, join the drama club, and start getting out there. The faster you get out there, the better you will start to feel. Believe me. I am loving life right now, and I am so excited for college. I am here to tell you it gets better. You are not alone. Fight for love.

Love,

Your Older Self (written with The Bully Teacher)

Author's Note: The second letter was a visualization exercise we did to create some hope and gain insight about what brings the Unlovable Self joy. The student wrote this letter with some prompts and re-read it to herself every day. We are glad to announce that she is a healthy teenager, on the honor roll, and in love with an amazing partner.)

Dear Unlovable Self

This is the Bully Teacher. You have enough outside noise judging you. Don't let your inner self be destroyed. Your parents' divorce is not your fault. Your mom cheated on your dad. He found out and blames you for not telling him. That's messed-up!

I am here to tell you, as a parent and Bully Teacher, that your dad needs some love and some help. You're twelve years old, living in a battle zone. Your parents forgot that they were supposed to be the adults. They're in so much pain that they don't see the harm that was transferred to you. That's not your fault. This situation is out of your control, but there are a few things you can do to help yourself.

Talk to your parents (separately) and tell them how you feel. If that's too scary, then write them a letter and share how you feel. If that's too much, then journal or write a letter to get all that pain out of your beautiful heart. Get those painful words out of your head and onto paper. Journal every day about your pain, be creative, and let it out.

Don't stuff your pain down, because it won't go away. If you keep stuffing the pain away, you'll think of ways to escape it. Then you'll be tempted to fall into the wrong crowd or indulge in risky behaviors that really will impact your future. You don't want that. All you want is for the pain to stop. Get the pain out, find something you love to do, and put your heart into it. It might be joining the drama troupe and being in a play, or joining a sport, or taking part in an after-school club. Commit to one thing and show up, because the other people involved in it will be counting on you.

I recommend that you also talk to your counselor. She has so many resources, and she would love to help you. She's a good listener, and I think you need someone to just listen to you. I promise that divorce sucks but that life gets better. I hope that one day you see that amazing girl standing in front of the mirror, looking back at herself, loving what she sees. We all see it at Bulldog.

With so much love and positivity,

The Bully Teacher

Middle School Letter, 8th Grade: Self-Esteem and Body Shaming

Dear Bully,

I hate myself and am scared to come to school because of you. I know I'm taller and bigger than the other girls in the class, but this is my body, this is me. You always whisper behind my back when I come to school, and tell everyone that I am, "so fat" and "look like a football player", it really hurts. You don't know that I cry at night, or whenever I'm in the shower I pray to be smaller like you and the other girls. I hate myself. I stand in front of the mirror everyday and pull at my skin and fat wishing I could cut it off. I know you and everyone hates me because of my weight, I hate myself too. I wish you would stop, or take the chance to get to know me... and not my weight.

Tall Girl

Dear Tall Girl,

It upsets me that you feel this way. No one should ever be afraid to go to school or feel as if their weight is something that defines them. I understand that the bully's comments hurt. Weight is something that's relative, and height is something that you cannot change. What matters most is how you feel about yourself. Truth be told, I dealt with these same issues when I was your age, and I still sometimes deal with them from time to time now. I'm 5' 9" and larger for my frame. I'm almost always one of the biggest girls in the room, in terms of height, weight, or both. Most of us are self-critical, no matter what shape, size, or age we are. But throughout the years, I've definitely found strategies that helped me address these issues. Maybe these strategies will work for you.

I remind myself that, although I'm bigger, I'm also strong. My thicker body has given me space for thicker muscles and has allowed me to compete and excel in college sports. Although I'm bigger and I can grab the bigger parts of my body, just like you, I have a better fitness level than people smaller than I am. What has your body allowed you to do that other people can't? It can be as simple as reaching the top shelf in your closet.

Confidence has also helped me, but confidence is found in different ways. I used to feel confident when I was playing soccer, but I no longer play organized sports. It may sound silly, but these days, I make myself feel confident by the way I dress. I make sure I put together outfits that make me feel powerful. I live according to the saying, "Look good, feel good." Feeling confident on the outside starts to change the attitudes you have on the inside. When you dress to your liking, you're more likely to give yourself positive affirmations: "I look good" or "I look beautiful." These affirmations stick with you as you leave your house.

Find that thing that makes you feel confident. It may not be sports, and it may not be fashion. When do you feel most confident? Channel that energy and let it shine! Try out those positive affirmations, too! You may not truly believe them, but you can trick yourself into feeling them.

Once you feel more confident in yourself, you may feel inspired to address the bully. If you choose to do this, I advise you to keep it short and simple: "I don't know what I ever did to you, but what you say about me feels terrible. Your criticism doesn't end at school. I take it home with me. I need you to stop." Maybe you haven't found that confidence yet, and that's ok. You should still tell a trusted adult—a parent or school counselor—about the girl who makes the comments. They'll help you through the struggles you face and may be able to have a conversation with that girl.

Being confident in your skin is something that's not going to happen overnight. It's something that I still struggle with. We strive for more good days than bad days.

In closing, I leave you with two quotes from Ashley Graham, the confident, plus-size model: "Confidence is not something that happens overnight. I have been working on it for a long time. I look in the mirror and do affirmations: 'You are bold,' 'You are brilliant,' 'You are beautiful.'" And "At the end of the day, what I want women to know is that beauty comes in all different shapes and sizes. And it should not define who you are."

I believe in you. You are beautiful!

Sending you love and positivity,

The Bully Teacher

Stop and Think

Self-esteem and Self-perception

Throughout middle and high school, a child's self-esteem can be like a yo-yo. With change comes an adjustment period. Bullying or harassment take a toll on a child's self-worth and self-esteem. We want to build our children's resilience and self-love and help them during this time of transition. Daily practices and emotional tools can help build a positive wall that protects a child from self-destructing. A bully does not bully a wall; they choose a target. We want to help our children be able to withstand judgments, whispers, rumors, and gossip and to reflect them back to the bully with no residual impact. If children don't believe something about themselves, then they don't own it.

For example, we worked with a mother who told us that based on the stories her child brought home, she worried that he was being bullied. One day, she decided to go to the school to see what was happening. She watched her child on the playground with other kids. At first, their interactions seemed really normal. She was about to leave when an event caught her attention. A boy called her son and the friend he was playing with "stupid losers," then proceeded to say, "You can't play with us, you freaks!" In panic mode, the mother attempted to find a recess monitor. But then, something great happened. Her son turned to the boy and said, "Dude, we are not stupid" and laughed at him. He and his friend walked away confidently and joined another group playing ball. The bully stood there dumbfounded; he had just gotten served. The son hadn't cared about the bully's words; he hadn't even flinched when he'd heard them. He hadn't believed that he or his friend were stupid or freaks, so they walked away from that interaction unscathed. He had shown confidence and put up a wall to protect himself and his friend.

We can visualize this idea another way. If someone on a project at work called us a "banana," would we own it? Would we feel like a banana for the rest of the day? No, we would probably think that at some point they had lost their minds, and we would move on.

Our point is to teach children that words only have power if we give it to them. A word can wound only if it carries weight for a child. By focusing on our children's strengths, and building positive affirmation throughout our homes, sharing gratitude and gifting kindness, we give our children an opportunity to truly see the best side of this world.

Building confident children with strong self-esteem is critical for their emotional development. When a child has strong self-esteem and confidence, they are more resilient and able to adapt to change. They are self-assured and are less likely to get involved in risky behaviors that might impact their health, future, or safety.

Self-esteem Builder

Below are some simple strategies that we have alluded to earlier in the book (in the elementary school section), but we want to elaborate on them more and give parents and teachers insight to gain a better understanding of a teenage mind. These strategies can be used to help our children understand their worth and to celebrate their differences. They can help build self-esteem and self-worth.

- Modeling confidence within ourselves: We all pick on ourselves sometimes, but we should choose to model our own body confidence to our teens. We might feel old, fat, ugly, stupid, stuck, unseen, or tired. But we should add positive momentum to those feelings. We should wake up each day and shout, "I am beautiful. I feel strong. Today is a good day. I love my life. I am grateful for my home and my children." We can spin negative thoughts into a positive whirl once in a while. We have nothing to lose. If we wake up stressed, tired, and hating our jobs, there is no good energy following us. This negativity flows right onto our children. We should wake up and make it a new day. Make the day how we want it to be. There is nothing to lose with positive thoughts. At the end of the day, we can hardly blame our positive thoughts for ruining our day. Although we might fall into the FAN syndrome, our positive thoughts start to shift our own thinking and, in turn, shift our children's thoughts about themselves. Our thoughts carry us so far every day. We make decisions based on our thoughts, and we have about a gazillion a day, so we ought to start with positive ones once in a while. Our thoughts are so powerful, driving our emotions and impacting our behaviors. We can imagine how our days would be if we were able to start them on a positive note.
- Being more aware of the words surrounding our bodies. Mothers who have a few stretch marks from birthing children should learn to celebrate them in front of their teens. "You see these lines? They're my tiger stripes. I earned these because my body did something wonderful and created you. You're the best thing that ever happened to me." Or "When I look at my stripes, they remind me of how my body was able to create you. I see you, and I'm so proud." Those are really powerful words to talk about how we are connected to our children. They also diminish the idea of our bodies as vessels and show that they are perfect. We should talk about all the imperfections.
- Trying not to talk about our own weight or size and trying not to compare our current selves to our past selves in front of our teens. It never helps a child to talk

about the fact that we used to be skinny and now we are fat. Girls want to associate themselves with mothers. They often feel like "mini-mes," and when they hear harsh words of hate or despair about their mother's bodies, they learn to own them. We also discourage to the highest degree a mother comparing herself to her teen, as this kind of comparison only fuels pain. We recommend that parents think about their triggers and how they might impact their children. Weight is a huge issue for teen girls, and we mostly see it arise in mother/daughter relationships.

- Talking about times when, as parents, we had to be brave and step out of our own comfort zone. We can talk about a time we did something that was really scary, like public speaking or trying out for something. We can relate the story to our children. Children love stories and gain a lot of insight from how their parents processed their experiences.
- Sharing stories of times when we, as parents, had to build our confidence. Not only will these stories set an example for our teens, but they will also build deeper connections between parents a children. We can talk about times when we had to stand up for ourselves or for someone else and about how scared we were or the fact that we didn't know what would happen. We can explain that we played out the situation a million times in our heads and talk about our feelings and how our bodies reacted. We should build the context so that children can relate to and see themselves in the story.
- Developing positive self-talk, using the "I am" statements we have mentioned in the earlier chapters of this book. We can make these statements a habit every night—saying them right before bed, at the dinner table, or in passing—or we can write them in the morning. All parents can do this. They can make it a game or a funny, cheesy thing they do. We can walk around and state what makes us amazing. It is a great tool to bring the positive back into our homes. In our office, we use positive ramping. When we have a bad day, we go around and list all the stuff that is good in our life, all the stuff we love about ourselves, and the stuff we look forward to. We like to ramp just like we like to vent. Instead of venting, we ramp about what we love.
- Teaching our children about self-acceptance and self-improvement and explaining these concepts to them. For example, our teens may be struggling to master a skill, and they might say they will never be able to learn it, they will always suck, they aren't smart enough. This kind of talk will forever be a problem. It is the FAN syndrome again. We must address it and correct it.
- Explaining to our teens that it is ok to accept flaws (We all have them!), but we must focus on our strengths. They should try and make the effort to do their best, instead of worrying about the outcome of being the best. We can teach them to accept their flaws, because we have unlimited resources to help us when we get stuck. If a weakness comes to the surface, we can help them find a resource to overcome it. Most importantly, we should not focus on the negatives. An abundance of resources can help us with whatever problem we have; we just have to ask for help.
- Praising our teens' effort, as opposed to the outcome of the event, whether our teen succeeds or doesn't succeed. We can show our teen it is ok if they "fail," because the important part is the effort that they made. Instead of talking about the grade they got on an exam, for example, we can praise them for all the studying they did. "That

chemistry exam was really hard. I know you wanted a higher grade, but you put so much effort into studying for it, and for that I'm very proud of you. I couldn't have done what you did. I'm so proud that you took on that test. You did your best." We should focus on the effort, versus the outcome.

The important part is to find our child's strength zone and foster what will build them up. These are some strategies that we hope provide more ideas for building a child up for greatness.

The Dangerous 3S: Self-Harm, Suicide Ideation, and Self-Hate

3S behaviors are self-destructive behaviors that stem from past experiences, trauma, bullying, or peer pressure. In our programs and across the nation, we have seen a rise in suicide ideation, self-hate, and self-harm behaviors, mostly in middle school, but they can easily trickle into high school. We often hear:
- "I hate myself."
- "My parents wouldn't even notice if I wasn't here anymore."
- "I think I'm depressed."
- "I feel a release when I cut myself."
- "My scars match the pain that I feel inside."
- "I don't think anyone would miss me if I die."
- "The world would be a better place without me."
- "I'm a mistake."
- "I'm not good enough."
- "I'm a loser."
- "I hate my body."
- "I don't want to live anymore."
- "I want to kill myself."
- "I'm under so much stress. I just want it to stop."
- "I can't fail. I just can't fail... Failing is not an option."
- "I need to be the best. I have to be the best."
- "If my parents find out, it's the end of me."
- "I'm terrified to disappoint my parents."
- "I hate the pressure and stress. I want to disappear."
- "No one understands me or gets me. I am alone."
- "I wish I was never born."
- "I have no friends, and I hate my life."

These statements are all from middle school kids. They feel stuck under a lens, judged and criticized by peers, by their online followers, and by us as parents and educators. When a child in middle school feels like they have no outlet or connection to their world, they might indulge in self-destructive behaviors or dangerous activities, to fill that void. They move into self-judgment and self-hate. Too many kids think negative thoughts about themselves, and we want to put a stop to these thoughts.

Building self-esteem in middle school can help create more positive self-perception, healthier behaviors or habits, and less inclination to indulge in risky behaviors. Some of the riskier and more dangerous behaviors we see in middle school are the following:
- Sexting
- Engaging in unprotected sexual activities
- Vaping
- Using drugs and Alcohol
- Performing dangerous stunts
- Self-mutilating (cutting) and having suicide ideations

We should approach conversations about these issues with openness and compassion. We want to create a safe place to explain the *why*, the consequences, and the lasting impact of these self-destructive behaviors. We want to stay away from judgment, blame, or strong egotistical standpoints.

Sexting. We know it is hard to think that a sixth grader would send nudes to their peers, but it happens more than we want to admit. We need to talk to our children about this self-destructive behavior and about the severe consequences that can negatively derail their bright academic or athletic futures. We have so many stories about nude photos going viral and traveling between our children's phones and tablets in sixth, seventh and eighth grades. Sadly, the stories never end happily. Children and parents get branded as sexual predators or convicted of child pornography. The exposed child gets slut-shamed, ridiculed, and harassed. Getting caught in the crossfire of a sexting war can be seen as social suicide. These horrific situations start and escalate with a frequency that can easily make anyone sick to their stomach. Below are some stories that tend to cycle through middle school:

Exhibit A: A boy likes a girl, and they are "talking," "dating," or "boyfriend/girlfriend." They spend hours texting back and forth, sharing lots of secrets and getting to know each other. They feel connected. One Saturday, the boy invites his friends over, and he starts sharing the texts from his girlfriend. One of his friends calls him lame and pressures him into asking more riskier questions like, "Would you rather…" Then, they go a step farther, and his friends start pressuring him to share funny emojis such as the peach, the eggplant, and the splashing water image, which all have sexual connotations.

The girl is sitting in her room with friends, excited and giddy. Her bedroom door is closed, so all her parents can hear is laughing, giggling, and playful screaming. The girls are excited about the attention from the boys and feel riskier as time passes. Then, with all the peers around, pressuring the new couple, a dare evolves as the pictures, memes, and gifs are no longer exciting to them. The behavior escalates, and the kids don't know how to walk away. Their behavior rises to a new level of risk. Then, someone asks the other for a naked picture…

Exhibit B: A girl used to date a boy. The relationship was short-lived, but to the girl, it seemed to last an eternity. During that romantic phase, the boy asked for a picture (a sexy one), so he could keep it close to him and have it all the time. He promised he would never share it and said that it would really make him so happy. The girl wanted to please her boyfriend and was afraid to lose him if she didn't send a picture. She kept thinking about how popular he was and the fact that all the other girls liked him. She really believed that "he can replace me fast if he wanted." She pulled her shirt up and snapped a shot. Three weeks later, they broke up, and he started dating Lily. Lily went through his phone and found the picture. She got jealous and shared it with all her friends...

Exhibit C: A boy started sending sexy texts of desire to his girlfriend. He asked a lot of questions about sex and what would she be willing to do. He had been caught at school with porn, so he had seen a lot more than she had ever experienced. He wanted her to show him how much she cared about him and he started putting more and more pressure on her. He texted, "If you don't send me pics, then I don't think you really love me. You say all this stuff and it's all talk. I'm starting to think you're a prude." He sent her a picture of his penis to start the process going, and things escalated.

Exhibit D: A couple is dating, and they start making out behind the bleachers. Things get hot and heavy. The girl goes down on the boy, he pulls out his phone, and films the sexual act. He then shows the video to all his friends to show off.

These are all true stories that Bulldog has seen in middle school and high school. Regardless of our thoughts about the appropriate age to be sexually active, naked pictures are being snapped in middle school. It is better to have a conversation about this topic sooner, rather than later. Below are topics to cover and explore when addressing sexting with middle and high school students.

- Be clear about what can happen when children take a naked picture or share one.
- Explore how it would feel if everyone saw a naked picture of them.
- Go over the severe consequences of sharing naked pictures.
    - Criminal charges
    - Child pornography charges
    - Sexual predator tags
    - Loss of scholarships
    - Denial of high school applications
    - Limited college eligibility
    - Branding online forever because of the incidents
- Talk about the fact that a child can be held accountable for a picture that ends up on their phone or tablet, even if they didn't take it or share it.
- Tell children not to take anyone's pictures or video without their consent.
- Tell children not to make sex videos.
- Remind children not to take any footage of any friends naked, even as a joke.
- Tell children that if someone is pressuring them to send a nude, they should say no. They should learn to stand up for themselves and feel safe within a romantic relationship.
- Tell children to report to a trusted adult if nudes are circulating.

We should be aware of these games that, in middle school, can lead to unwanted sexual misconduct:

- Truth or dare (There are risky dares on certain apps.)
- Rainbow game
- Spin the bottle (There are a many of apps for this game.)
- Strip poker
- Choking game
- Vampire biting
- Chat Roulette.com

We recommend that teachers and parents start discussing sexting in sixth grade. They should talk about the fact that children might be curious about their bodies and might see provocative videos or pictures online that they find sexy, beautiful, or funny. Curiosity about nudity or sexual orientation is normal.

Vaping. The use of vape pens or e-cigarettes is on the rise. To our children, these products seem like safer, but still rebellious, alternatives to actual smoking. Vaping appeals to teens because it can be done anywhere and fairly secretly. Vape pens are becoming easier and easier for teens to access. They are sold in gas stations and drug stores.

The problem is the limited research into and lack of knowledge about vaping. One fear about vaping is that we do not know all of the ingredients in a cartridge or serum. Vaping is fairly new, and we are just starting to understand some of the effects that it may have on our respiratory systems and bodies. The public learned for the first time about the links between vaping/e-cigarettes and death in 2019.

We must educate ourselves about vaping and understand its dangers. We should have open conversations about vaping with our middle school children. It is better to have these conversations earlier, rather than later. By sharing what we have learned about the negative impact vaping can have on our health, we might help children resist peer pressure.

Drugs and Alcohol. Most people may anticipate that their children will explore drugs and alcohol at some point in high school. However, we have seen a rise in drug and alcohol consumption in seventh and eighth grades. We should have conversations about substance abuse in middle school and give our children transition statements to overcome peer pressure.

Below are some transition statements for children to use if faced with peer pressure to do drugs or drink alcohol. These statements allow children not to feel totally lame or get picked on because they are saying no to drinking and drugs.

- "I can't drink tonight. My mom is picking me up, and she's going to check me."
- "I have a big game/practice tomorrow. I can't drink or smoke."
- "My coach is drug testing us."
- "My school tests for nicotine, drugs, and alcohol at random."
- "I don't feel like drinking tonight."
- "I'm on antibiotics, and I can't mix them with alcohol."

- "I'm allergic to beer or hard alcohol. I turn red, and I get really hot."
- "My parents are on my back. I can't risk getting caught."
- "I have a ton of addiction in my family. I can't risk trying alcohol or drugs."
- "It's not my thing. I'm cool for now."
- "I'll pass. I'm tired/wiped out."
- "I'm not staying long. My parents are picking me up."
- "My older brother and sister just got busted, so I need to lay low for now."

Dangerous Stunts. We have also seen a rise in children attempting dangerous stunts to mimic YouTube stars. Often, teens want some sort of challenge or thrill, and they might use dangerous dares to fulfill this desire, engaging in harmful activities that can affect their future or safety. Our children often see these videos and want to reenact them. The danger is when they take action and follow through on the stunts. Some kids get bullied into challenges or pranks.

We should talk about these stunts or dares and how they can really be dangerous. We should have conversations about pranks and dares and how peers can pressure us into doing things that can be painful or dangerous. We should talk about the dangers and about ways children can step away from harmful situations. We can give them strategies to avoid these activities and have them visualize situations and play them out. The goal is to give them one-liners or comebacks to help when they feel pressure to participate in dangerous pranks.

In our groups, we have found that more boys tend to engage in stunts that can be harmful, such as:
- Waging prank wars
- Jumping off buildings or bridges
- Having water gun fights with boiling water
- Eating dog food instead of real food
- Doing the eraser or deodorant challenge
- Doing the Tide Pod Challenge
- Car surfing
- Stealing a pizza from a delivery guy using a toy gun

If a child is a thrill-seeker, we can find activities to help them feel fulfilled without harming themselves. The following are some thrill-seeking activities to suggest:
- Mountain biking
- Rock climbing
- Boxing
- Surfing or windsurfing
- Going to theme parks
- Playing paintball
- Riding bumper cars
- Doing an escape room
- White water rafting

- Sailing
- Doing a polar plunge
- Exploring new cities or places
- Skydiving

Suicide Ideation and Self-Mutilation. We are not experts when it comes to suicide ideation or self-mutilation. However, over the years, during our programs, we have had to discuss this topic over and over. Sometimes, a child is in so much emotional pain that they find a release by matching that emotional pain with physical pain. They use cutting as a form of release from the pressure and pain that they hold inside. At other times, the self-harm is a group activity. We have sat in groups where there was an epidemic of self-harming behaviors in seventh grade. In one particular case, we found that self-mutilation was a game, a dark and twisted game in which the group would cut their wrists, legs, chest, and feet and then share images in a private group on social media. The members of the group would compare their experiences to see who had the worst life.

Here are some sample narratives to use with our children if they are harming themselves:

Sample A: "Honey, thanks for sharing this with me. You're in so much pain. Tell me more about the pain. I see you crumbling, and you keep me so far away. How can I connect with you? What can I do to help?"

Sample B: "Thanks for trusting me with this. It seems like your pain is really deep, and you might need some help or support. Are you open to talking to someone or going to a support group? I'm here for you, and I want you to feel safe. I also want you to find that spark, the joy that you're missing or that left you. What is one small thing we can do, starting today?

The goal is to go through the following process and hit the points below. We should:
- Share the different emotions that come up.
- Discuss the child's thoughts surrounding the emotions.
- Talk about the behaviors or the incident that initiated the self-mutilation.
- Talk about what the child wants for themselves.
- Ask about what we can do.
- Ask about what they can do.
- Ask about what steps they want to take.
- Recap and agree to the next steps.
- Share gratitude and care for the fact that they opened up.

We often hear children say that they hate their lives and wish they didn't exist. They say they are a disappointment or a waste of a life. We often ask if middle school teens have ever thought of suicide, and more often than we ever anticipated, they share that they have thought about it.

Thinking about suicide does not necessarily mean that children are a danger to themselves. Talking about suicide also does not increase the chances of a child taking their own life. These thoughts are worrisome and need to be addressed, but in a loving, supportive way.

We should educate our children about mental wellness and about better addressing the signs of depression. Often, these uncomfortable conversations with our children open doors to better understand their emotional states and to feel more connected to them. We can also give them the tools to help their friends or peers.

The following are some signs of suicide ideation or depression:
- Experiencing isolation
- Feeling hopeless, trapped, or stuck
- Talking about death or suicide
- Not talking about the future
- Giving away meaningful possessions
- Engaging in risk-taking behaviors
- Abusing substances more frequently
- Focusing on death or a means to kill themselves
- Allowing grades to slip and changing behavior
- Acting as though this is their last day, sharing goodbyes
- Exhibiting a high level of anxiety
- Showing changes in behavior
- Disengaging with friends and activities
- Feeling deep-rooted shame and helplessness
- Experiencing recurring and inescapable bullying or trauma
- Losing sight of the big picture and focusing on the pain

There is no one telltale sign for suicide ideation. We must notice a change in behavior and listen to the child. What is different? What emotions do they project? How are they acting?

We need to focus our love and parenting by opening our hearts to difficult conversations. We need to work on talking about the 3S syndrome and teaching our children about self-love.

Chapter 20: The Cycle of Bullying

Middle School Letter, 7th Grade: Bully/Victim Cycle

Dear Bully,

The other day at the park you were making fun of me and being racist. You were calling me names, threatening to fight me, calling me a pussy, a fag, and imitating me. I saw your post on Snapchat. What have I ever done to you?

I tried to act cool, but I was really getting hurt and sad. Then you lied. You told your mom and our teacher at our school that I pushed you and that I was making fun of you. Now your mom is constantly picking on me, putting me down, or making an example of me. She's eyeballing me and pointing at me. It is annoying and I can't prove that I am right. What's your beef with me? I have never done anything to you. Get off my back!

Targeted

Dear Victim,

I know that I lied and I do attack you when I get a chance. I know I won't get caught because of my mom. This is hard for me to admit and I will deny I ever wrote this. I will tear this letter up but I need to say this first.

I feel this sense of power and I want to hurt you as much as you hurt me. Remember, I am sure you forgot, but I didn't. You uninvited me from your party in front of our class, called your mom and said that I hurt you. She called my mom, and no one believed me. I was considered a bully, a snitch, and a loser in 3rd grade. I lost all my friends and played the rest of the year alone on the playground. My mom told me to never trust anybody and that I don't need anyone. She is right!

So I don't see why you can't take it if you were able to dish it out. Don't play the victim when you got away with bullying me for years.

The Bully

Dear Bully/Dear Victim,

There is so much pain in both these letters that I need to step in and share some of my thoughts. You were both in the wrong at some point. That does not mean that there is a line in the sand, and you can't cross over it to figure out how you can start to heal. You used to be best friends, and now, I see the divide between you and am hoping we can mend your relationship.

Forgiveness is not weak. It's a sign of strength. You might not believe me now, but once you forgive and let go of all that resentment, you feel stronger. I'm not calling you out and do not want to get either of you in trouble, but we need to come to an understanding.

You are both hurt and in a lot of pain. From working with you, I know that you both come from difficult homes. Your dads are absent, and each of your mothers has a bucket of problems. You have shared those facts in group with me on multiple occasions. But it's not cool for either of your mothers to gang up on you. They need to stop, because they can get into a lot of trouble and cause your rift to escalate to new heights. Moms should never go after another child. That never ends well.

You are also at a crossroads here. You're finishing up middle school, and I see that you are hanging around the wrong crowd—both of you! I know that you're in the initial phases of being recruited by gangs. You act all cool and sly in my classes, but from your journals and during our one-on-one, I can tell that you're terrified. So I am pleading with you to think about your futures, about high school, about an opportunity to go to college, about building a lives for yourselves out of this neighborhood.

I see the potential in both of you and how great you both are when you put your guards down and really open up. You can get scholarships for basketball, soccer, or baseball. You're both talented athletes. You keep circling around gangs and violence, and I wish I could pull you both out of this.

I know teachers are hard on you, and you've developed shields to protect yourselves from being hurt. By doing this, you close yourselves off to love, care, and support. I disagree with your mother, Bully. Everyone needs to trust someone, and in order to thrive, we need people in our lives. I can't change what your mothers believe, but I can challenge their beliefs. We all need love; we all need to be cared for. I know that it has been a long time since you both felt unconditional love, and that brings me so much pain. When you feel love, you feel like you can accomplish anything, you feel safe, you feel supported, and you feel joy.

I want you to think really hard about a time you felt safe and loved. I want you to think about how that felt. Go back and remember those feelings. That's what I want you to feel every day.

You don't ever have to prove yourselves to me. I know you're both "tough" on the outside. It's the inside that worries me. I see the fear, pain, and resentment in your eyes. In our sessions, I just pray that I can get you to connect to the words I am sharing or connect to a story, so I can slowly pull you out of this cycle of violence. I tell you this every session: I believe in you, I see you, I hear you, and I'm here for you. Don't give up on yourselves, and please leave the attitude at the door and forgive each other. It's time you both got on the same side, so you find out what true friendship and forgiveness might look like. I can't change the world you live in, but I can try to help you shift perspectives and see a world that you can look forward to.

Sending you love and positivity,

The Bully Teacher

Middle School Letter, 8th Grade: The Cycle of Bullying

Dear Bully,

I've been bullied a lot throughout my years of living on this world, especially at this school. I think that because of me being bullied that caused me to be a bully. Sometimes I can be a bully but I think I've learned and reflected on myself as being a bully.

Reflecting on Myself

Dear Reflecting on Myself,

It sounds like you're at a turning point in understanding how your emotions impact your actions. Being bullied for years can take a toll on your body and mind. That pain and anger can just sit with you, especially if you don't feel safe talking about them. The pain doesn't just go away if you don't have the tools to get rid of it. It sits with you and, sadly, starts to define you. You might enter a room and feel like all eyes are on you.

Once a week, at your school, we see you, we hear you. We know it's hard to go through our program. You often get targeted, and when we come in, you can be resistant to working with us. You respond by being mean in order to protect yourself. I would do the same thing. Your pain feels debilitating, and we understand. Believe me, the world is not against you. I have felt what you feel, and it's the *worst*. But you need to see the other side of all this mess.

I want you to start letting go of your anger, by first forgiving yourself. None of this was your fault. This all started when you just tried to protect yourself. You didn't know how to reach out for help. You were told snitches get stitches. You didn't know that there are adults who care. Your parents told you to defend yourself with your fists, but that isn't the solution and never will be. I get very mad when a parent tells a child to defend himself with violence. Think about it... Do you think your mom or dad go to work with their fists clenched, ready to fight? No! They would be fired.

We react to pain; we don't like it. When we feel pain, we need to learn to communicate and use our feelings as power. When you're angry, talk about your anger, instead of fighting. Walk away, breathe, or even go play basketball. Just change your environment first, then think about why you're so angry. Don't pick on the people who are easy targets because you can relate to their pain. I know you; you would never want to go to sleep knowing that you hurt someone so badly they cried themselves to sleep. You're so amazing and special. Your anger is directed at the wrong target. We want you to fuel your anger towards your passion. You're talented, and we believe in you. Don't forget to believe in yourself.

With love and tons of positivity,

The Bully Teacher
High School Letter, 9th Grade: Changing Schools, Changing Mindset

Dear Bulldog,

I wish I never came to this school because when I came to this school, my life changed. I started hanging out with people that weren't really people I ever thought I would hang out with. I started getting bad grades, I started to fight which almost cost me to be jumped but now when I decide to change, I feel like my past is catching up to me. I lived on the westside my whole life. I have been shot at before and robbed at gunpoint. I never grew up with my father there because he was always in and out of prison. I had to learn by myself how to fight and make my own money. And I hate it when these kids act like gang bangers because it's not a game or a joke and I had to learn that the hard way. And now my dean and parents aren't making it better.

Miss. Understood

Dear Miss. Understood,

I am sorry you're having a difficult time transitioning into your new school. I can only empathize with you about the experiences that you've been through. I can imagine they were very scary and stressful. You're turning a page to a new chapter, and I'm excited for you to make this start. From your letter, I gather that you have enough self-awareness to realize how the situation in your new school is impacting you. Being aware is half the battle. Now it's time to make the change that you seem to want so badly.

You have the ability to change your relationships with your deans and parents, but know that it's going to take dedication and time. The molds we initially cast for people are difficult to break. But if you're committed to the change, the adults in your life will see that you're trying. You can show your commitment by being accountable in the classroom and showing respectful behavior to all adults. We cannot control how other people see us, but we can control our actions and how we see ourselves. If you see yourself in a certain way, it's only a matter of time until others see you that way as well.

As for your classmates, I can see how it's triggering for someone to glamorize a life that's not glamorous at all. Being in a gang is not a matter of being "thug" or not; it is/was a way of survival. Many people will never understand that. When you see others acting like gangbangers, I encourage you to remove yourself from the situation. If one day, you feel like you can confront someone in a constructive way, I advise you to do that. Maybe start the conversation by saying, "I don't think it's very funny at all."

I leave you with this: we cannot control where we came from, but we can always change our fates. We can write a new chapter and create our ideal happy ending. Please remember that tough times don't last, but tough people do. If you're truly willing to make a change, I know that nothing will hold you back. I believe you can do whatever you put your mind to.

Sending strength your way,

The Bully Teacher

High School Letter, 11th Grade: The Cycle of Bullying

Dear Bulldog,

I have been bullied in 7th grade. I had really bad eyebrows and was always told that they looked like raccoon tails or something. The person who would make fun of my eyebrows did it behind my back and in person. I have also bullied people as well. In second grade me and someone else bullied this girl who used to go to my school. I felt bad and eventually apologized to her. We are friends now.

Eyebrows

Dear Beautiful Brows,

Your "raccoon tails" are beautiful. The stunning Cara Delevingne, who is known for her thick and dark eyebrows, states that, "The more we embrace who we are as people and rely less on our physical attributes, the more empowered we become. Beauty shouldn't be so easily defined. It is limitless." You are beautiful just the way you are.

When you admit that you have bullied someone, it shows that you are self-aware and know that you hurt the person. Self-awareness is a great attribute to have, and it leads to admitting when you are wrong or when you have hurt someone. It is wonderful that you two were able to become friends and move past the hurt.

You can use certain strategies to develop self-awareness. I've used some of them to remind myself of the importance of self-awareness in my daily life. The strategies are the following:

1. Try to look at yourself objectively. This helps, because you're not looking from the inside out, but from the outside in. You're able to see yourself and your actions through another's eyes.

2. Keep a journal, and in this journal, I write about how you feel each day and why you feel that way. Write down your goals and plans to achieve those goals.

3. Talk to friends who love and trust you and ask them to describe you. Seeing yourself through their eyes will give you a better perspective of yourself.

High School Letter, 12th Grade: Emotion Management

Dear Bulldog,

I realize that because this issue didn't seem like a big deal to make fun of one of my peers during group because he is a bully and you might not feel the same way about my approach to handling that situation. I was not trying to cause any trouble, I just wanted him to shut up. I realize that you might think it is a big deal. I respect that. I am sorry for my actions... I let the heat of the moment get to me. He irritates me, he talks over you, and bullied the Freshmen. I hope you can forgive me and we can move on.

Not a Big Deal

Dear Not a Big Deal,

I'm proud of you for recognizing that what you may not see as a big deal can be a big deal to someone else. It's important for us to be able to step out of our own shoes and try to step into someone else's to understand them and what may affect them. You said that you let the heat of the moment get to you. It's great that you were aware of your emotions in the moment, although you might not have wanted to react so emotionally at the time. It can be hard to address a situation when we are emotional, or "in the heat of the moment."

A few strategies can help you calm your emotions before you react to a problem or an issue. These work best with students your age:

1. Listening to music. Some students have mentioned that this is their best strategy. When they are upset at someone and know they need to calm down, they pop in their earbuds and have a jam session. Sing it out, shout it out, or dance it out before addressing the conflict.

2. Taking a nap. Do this only if you can (not during our program or class). If you get into a text or a phone argument with a friend, put the phone down and lie down for a bit. After a nap, you may feel better, and your head may be clearer. It only takes twenty minutes to reset.

3. Take a walk. If you're able to, get outside and leave your phone behind. Do it! Take a walk around the block and get some fresh air. During this time, thoughts may be running through your head, or you may be talking yourself through what just happened. This allows you to process the argument, understand why you are angry, and decide how you can address the situation calmly.

4. Remove yourself from the situation and distract yourself. Watch a show; find someone you can help; go work out; do something that will take your mind off the situation.

These are the top strategies that students have told us can help. What about you? What would be your best strategy? We hope our letter helps you. We are here to support you.

Sending you love and positivity,

Stop and Think

Trauma and Triggers

Psychological trauma is damage to the brain after a painful or stressful experience. Our trauma and painful experiences shape how we see and walk through the world. We often get so caught up in our own lives that we fail to realize that others might be in pain, too. In our groups, some teens hold onto trauma, painful experiences, or distressing memories as a defense mechanism, to remind themselves that they never want to be in those situations again. The traumatic stories we have heard can lead to aggressive outbursts, bullying, and violence.

When fear and anger fuel our brains, they can keep us from letting go of the past, trusting people, and pursuing new opportunities. While it is important to remember the past, it is not good to be consumed by it. As with all things, we begin to heal ourselves through self-awareness. Eventually, we have to let go of the hurt to move on.

A trigger is a thought, situation, conversation, behavior, or place that creates a strong negative emotional response. When we are aware of our triggers, we can stay emotionally balanced and address situations without emotional responses.

Letting Go of Trauma: Resentment and Forgiveness

We have found that the biggest challenges victims of trauma face are letting go of past memories, resentment, and forgiveness. Many children hold onto their painful memories or refuse to forgive the perpetrators. This accumulation of trauma creates an emotional imbalance and builds up a lot of negative self-talk and many protective strategies. Children who resent others and don't let go have a difficult time trusting; they fear being themselves, and they feel like they are constantly being judged.

In our groups, we have seen a clear decrease in trust over the years. Middle school children often struggle with trusting teachers and their peers. They can be driven by fear and past painful experiences. They don't want to look bad; they fear rejection; they want to fit in; they have visceral reactions to exclusion. They struggle to move past painful experiences and learn to build some resilience.

In our high school groups, students have often been burned and have naturally pivoted into a group or clique that they feel most identifies with them. They struggle to move out of their safety group and often distrust authorities, educators, and even their peers. They also struggle to see that they are not alone; most of their peers experience the same emotions that they do. They tend to be more and more connected to one another; however, they are also often more isolated from each other. We have seen a lot of backstabbing, lying, and exclusion.

Children have to move past uncomfortable events in order to live in the moment. To move forward, they need to let go and forgive, to give or accept an apology and truly mean it.

Easier said than done, right? Many people have accepted an apology, only to then bring up the incident again at a later date. It does not feel good when someone digs up past mistakes and throws them into our faces. We want to really work on forgiving, letting go, and accepting apologies.

Strategies to Practice Letting Go

A simple way to teach our children to practice letting go is to tell them that when they feel guilt, anger, or frustration, they should take a deep breath, put their hand on their hearts, and say, as they exhale, "I forgive myself for_____ and feeling_____. They can repeat this exercise until they release the negative emotion. By forgiving themselves first, they can more easily forgive others and learn to move on.

Sometimes, we have to do the apologizing, and that is difficult. It is hard to admit that we did something wrong or hurt someone. When our ego plays into our emotions, there can be a lot of resistance to admitting a wrongdoing. By focusing on the behavior and not our character, we apologize more easily. These ideas help our teens when we discuss these issues.

Examples of shifting from character mode into behaviors mode:
- Instead of saying, "I'm sorry I hurt you. I'm a bad person," shift to: "I'm sorry I hurt you. I lost my temper."
- Instead of saying, "I'm sorry I started the rumors about you. I'm bitter about...," shift to "I'm sorry I started the rumors about you. I was feeling jealous and reacted to my feelings."
- Instead of saying, "I'm sorry I called you a loser. I'm a mean person," shift to "I'm sorry I called you a loser. I was feeling hurt and said some mean stuff."

Another strategy to practice letting go is to talk about and play out a situation from start to finish. Sometimes all a child needs is to brain dump all the information without hearing a strategy. A good venting session can feel good.

Lastly, we cannot reiterate enough the art of journaling. Letting emotions out on paper is a release, and children don't need to hold back. Journaling is a powerful process.

To overcome conflict and painful emotions, we need to give our children the tools to forgive each other and themselves.

We have found that our teens struggle mostly with the "how" of letting go and moving on. Below are some ideas to work on letting go and forgiving others:

- Identify the emotions: Anger, fear, embarrassment, sadness, shame, jealousy, confusion, resentment, loneliness, or rage
- Find the behavior and thought connected to it: What are you thinking when these emotions come up? What do you end up doing or saying?
- Process the emotion so you can come up with solutions to get back into a better headspace: "I'm feeling angry, and I want to post something online, but I know that will just fuel the drama."
- Keep from replaying the situation over and over in your head: This feeds the negative emotions. Remember that replaying situations is not helpful. Delete and Don't Repeat.
- Talk to yourself when you feel as though you are focusing too much on the situation and giving it more attention than it deserves: Use statements like these:
    i. "I need to stop replaying this. It's not serving me."
    ii. "It isn't helping me to re-read all these comments."
    iii. "This isn't serving me."
    iv. "The story is only fueling anger, fear, and pain."
    v. "This isn't the story I want to replay in my head."
    vi. "I don't like how I'm thinking or feeling right now."
    vii. "I'm moving into a different room and walking away."
    viii. "This isn't helping me."
    ix. "I'm not letting this get to me."
    x. "This isn't on me."
    xi. "My ego is getting in the way."

Learning to apologize is so important to the process of letting go and healing. In most of our groups, teens don't know how to say, "I am sorry" and really mean it. They tend to skip the apology and just pretend everything is cool. The challenge is that over time, things are not cool, and resentment starts to bubble. By teaching our children how to apologize, we open doors to stronger and healthier relationships. Below are the simple steps to an apology.

Sincere apology:

- Step 1: Acknowledge the behavior: "I'm sorry for…"
- Step 2: Explain how it hurt: "I know it hurts you…" or "I know it stresses you…"
- Step 3: Make amends: "I will make this better by…" or "I will fix this by…"
- Step 4: Create change: "In the future I will…"

- **When apologizing, stay away from the following:**

- "I'm sorry, *but*…"
- "In all honesty, it wasn't all my fault."
- "I'm sorry that you're so sensitive."
- Blaming the person to whom you are apologizing
- Making the person feel bad or guilty as you apologize
- Giving excuses as you apologize
- Using backhanded compliments or jabs as you apologize

When helping our teens learn to let go and overcome resentment, we talk about learning to accept an apology and learning to move on. They need to learn how to forgive and let go. Sometimes it might take time, but they must be clear and truthful about their intentions when accepting an apology. If they need time, they can be honest and say that they appreciate the apology and need more time. They should also say, "I accept or appreciate your apology." They should never say, "It's ok." By saying "It's ok," they demean themselves. They are saying it is ok to be mistreated or hurt. They should use power statements when accepting an apology.

The following are examples of power statements:

- "I appreciate your apology."
- "I forgive you."
- "I'm grateful for our time talking about it. I accept your apology."
- "Thank you for apologizing. I accept your apology."
- "Thank you. I need a little time to process or get over it,"

Chapter 21: Slut-Shaming

The following section contains violent language. Please be advised.

Middle School Letter, 8th Grade: Sex Rumors

Dear Bully,

I heard this rumor about me. It is so untrue. I feel like everyone is looking at me. Believing what was shared. I didn't do it. I never did it. I am labelled as a slut. I am being slut shamed. I don't even know what that really means. I didn't do that stuff. I am finishing middle school and all the boys are laughing at me making sexual gestures. Why would you say that stuff about me? Now meme's are being spread about me. People are Snap chatting about me. I am alone and ashamed of something I didn't do. A boy the other day accused me of saying we slept together. I went to sleep away camp with him, but I never had sex with him. Why are these rumors being spread?

I thought things would be different in 8th grade. I hate myself right now. I am ashamed.

Dear Victim,

I've once spread a rumor without knowing it. Someone told me something and without knowing I told someone I thought knew. I did not realize it was not true. I thought it was funny, the more I think about it, I realize it is not. It is not common for 8th graders to do that stuff and you were at the party. They said there was a video of you. I didn't think that me sharing with someone else would have done this. My boyfriend told me and he thought it was funny. I guess I was kind of thinking it was ok to share. I didn't think about what it would do to you. Why were you under the bleachers? They said there was a video I just believe them. Now I see you being slut shamed. I am sorry. If I stand up to my boyfriend and his friends, I am afraid they will laugh at me. I don't trust people. I know you are hurting and I am sorry. I am sorry Ashter accused you of saying you slept with him. It was all Jacob's idea of a joke.

The Bully

Middle School Letter, 8th Grade: Racial Bullying and Slut-Shaming

Dear Bulldog,

I don't know what happened but all of a sudden I am a constant target to bullying by the black girls in my class. They use to at least be nice to me, now they are calling me skank, whore, and make fun of me. I don't know what happened. I just started dating Deon and the girls turned on me. They are mocking me on Snapchat, bullying me in the bathroom, shoving me in the hallways. Calling me spick and making hissing noises. I had a note in my locker saying they are going to call ICE on my family. They say I put out and the only reason Deon is with me is to get some because they aren't putting out. It is not true, I am not having sex. I have always liked Deon and I know he is the most popular boy in 8th grade, but he does not like these girls, he is into me. We were secretly dating for a while, and I wished we didn't go public. I hate going to school. I hate those girls, I just want to be with my boyfriend. I am afraid they will try to fight me. I can't snitch but I am tired of this crap.

Scared and Confused

Dear Scared and Confused,

There is so much that the teachers and I overlooked about this situation that I want to explore. As you know, I'm a white Canadian woman, and I only saw the surface of this bullying.

When I read your entry, I had to call one of my best friends. She's a beautiful, strong, brave, and intelligent black woman who mentors young black girls at her church. She is an incredible Reverend, and she's my "go-to person" when I don't quite understand multi-racial issues. My best friend shared the flip side of your story, and it started to make a lot more sense. She explained to me that in our culture, black women are constantly put down, compared, and criticized as they grow up. "Your butt is too big." "Your hair is to nappy." "Your skin is too dark." The media and our culture oppress young black women.

Deon is dating a Latina, and the black girls are hurt, jealous, and enraged because he went outside his own race to date you. This fact makes the girls feel like they are not good enough. They will never admit that they are hurt, because they're not aware of their own feelings of rejection and insecurity as a result of their own personal experiences. They are in pain because they make Deon's decision about their experiences and see it as a rejection of them. They internalize the pain they feel and project it onto you.

The emotional reaction of the girls is more than just a reaction to you and Deon. It's about a vicious racial divide and about the way we treat young black women. Therefore, none of this is your fault. The girls feel rejected and unworthy of love because Deon is dating you. In their anger, they target you. These are not conscious choices that they make; they are a reaction to their feelings.

Each culture has its triggers, and it seems that dating outside your own culture can really trigger young women. I share these facts only because I didn't know. I was at a loss for words when I heard your story. I thought I was witnessing a typical mean-girl attack, but the reasons for the behavior go so much deeper. I think that we need to talk about interracial dating and open communication about our feelings.

I'm sorry that you are being targeted and racially bullied. It's not right for these girls to attack you, and I'm here to help. This is not your fault.

I think there are a few things we can do.

1. Talk to the girls: I recommend that you figure out which girl is the most approachable and have a heart-to-heart with her when she is alone. Tell her that you want to understand what is going on and that you don't want any friction. Share how all this is hurting you and talk about the impact bullying has had on you. Ask how you can fix the situation or help to stop the bullying. By asking and trying to better understand the situation, you put your guard down. You open the door to connect and be real. By staying calm and dropping the attitude, you can get some good insight about what is going on.

2. Talk to your boyfriend: I know that eighth-grade love might not include talking about all this, but try to get some perspective. Deon might have some ideas or insights to stop this.

3. Be kind yet strong: Surround yourself with people who love and support you at recess, and before and after school. When the girls start to whisper or get in your face, make sure you are not alone. Get off of social media so you do not get looped into the drama. Be kind and helpful to your classmates. You will feel better, and you will build a stronger and stronger support system.

4. Find a counselor or teacher who might relate or who best understands you: I know your counselor, and she would be open to talking about racial bullying. She would also be a good ear to listen to your pain.

5. Start documenting the incidents: Write down details about the bullying; take snapshots of the online bullying; and add the dates, the account names, and the names of the girls involved. Then delete the online conversations and don't repeat them. In other words, don't re-read or replay the incidents. When you are ready, and I hope it is soon, you can give your bullying incident report to the principal. You will have concrete evidence to prove your case. I know you don't want to be a snitch, but you also want to protect yourself and salvage your self-worth. You might not be ready to report, but at least you will have documentation for when you feel brave enough to share a record of the harassment and bullying.

I'm here for you, and I can help by running girls' groups and talking about mending wounds and hurt. I don't want to take your power away or lose your trust, but I'm pushing you to report and get the help you need to feel safe. Just know and remember that you're doing nothing wrong. You have the liberty to date anyone that you want. Any relationship takes work, and dating interracially usually takes more. However, if you really care for each other, it will all work out, no matter what other people are saying to or about you.

Stay strong. Do you.

The Bully Teacher

Update: The girl talked to the counselor, documented incidents, and spoke to one of the girls. She was able to mend the relationship and keep the girls from getting suspended by doing some peace circles and talking about the impact of their actions. The principal assigned the girls after-school duties as a consequence and instructed the mean girls to mentor younger children. The healing process was long , but with restorative practices, the girls stayed in school and eliminated the threats.

High School Letter, 9th Grade: Sexual Name-Calling and Gossip

Dear Bully,

WTF with the drama at the party! Calling me a thot with your friends and laughing at me. You don't even know what happened. You didn't even ask me if I was ok. You just stood there and judged me. I thought you were different. I thought we were friends.

Never a Thot

Dear Victim,

I'm sorry for being mean to you behind your back. I mostly did it because you hurt my friend, and I wanted to defend her and that's the only way I know to be on her side. She said you hit on her boyfriend and Tiffany said you tried to kiss him.

I know you have said things about me behind my back, and on the camping trip you hurt my friend feelings again. That's why I laugh when they called you the school thot at the party. I'm really sorry about that. I know you think I started it, I didn't, but I did not stop it. I am sorry. I am starting to be afraid of what could happen to me, if I don't do what my friends do. I feel peer pressure to just be mean and that is not what I am about.

I am sorry and I will make it up to you,

The Bully

Stop and Think

Racial Bullying and Self-Image

Race is a social construct. Racial categories are man-made, and without any choice of our own, we are put into a category. In the entry above, the bullying was deeper than mean-girl drama. It was about self-image and self-worth. The girls were triggered, which brought up some past trauma or feelings, and they reacted by targeting the girl. This situation is about self-image, recognizing triggers, and being responsive to emotions.

Whatever a child is—Latina, black, or white—if they feel less-than or confused by how the media portrays them, they can develop challenging emotions and reactions. In this story, the girls got to explore self-image and how they often felt as though they were being defined by others. The girls talked about not feeling good enough and not pretty enough; "not enough" came through our peace circles. They had to reach a point where they felt valued and that they didn't need to let others define what they saw fit as beauty. They had to learn to stop the narrative of "She's not like me; she doesn't look like me..." When children start comparing and feeling inferior, they create an imbalance that messes with their emotions. The story had nothing to do with the boy; he was a subplot in the story.

These types of incidents need to be discussed more often, so young women can release some of the demons they carry.

Teachers, school administrators, and parents can stop these emotional imbalances by addressing them immediately. Often, they can simply ask "why" the behavior is happening on order to stop it, because the child usually does not know how to answer or does not have a just reason for why they are bullying someone because of their race. Parents and teachers can then discuss empathy, a "put-yourself-in-their-shoes" type of conversation: "How would it make you feel if…?"

This story also creates a segue to talk about interracial relationships, another tricky subject. Interracial dating can put a target on a romantic partnership because the two halves appear so different from the outside. In these discussions, it's important to be supportive, because there may be cultural differences among the children involved, but parents and teachers guide the child in learning about the new culture.

If we feel that a child is being bullied because they are in an interracial relationship, we can do the following:

1. Support them.
2. Put our biases aside.
3. Tell the child not to assume the worst when peers look or ask questions about their relationship.

Racial bullying and the bullying of interracial couples can be tough subjects to address when speaking to our children, but we can talk about these issues. We must remember to listen, be open, be honest, and never underestimate the power of teaching empathy and diverse thinking.

Slut-shaming

How to stop slut-shaming is a monumental question. This type of behavior is so deeply rooted in our society, and it has been around for years. Why is it only a label that applies to girls? It takes two to tango, and we often see boys participating in the same types of behavior. Slut-shaming is a way to take power from or establish control over a female. Why do we do it? It's a cycle that tarnishes self-image and self-perception and makes young ladies question their identity. ("Am I a slut? Is this not normal behavior?") Most so-called "slutty" behavior is normal behavior, and people are labeled because other people are jealous or upset. Because other people believe the "slut" label, it is difficult to overcome.

Chapter 22: Sexual Identity and Sexual Orientation

High School Letter, 11th Grade: Parental Pressure and Sexual Identity

Dear Bully,

I am your favorite target. Do you know how bad it hurts to get hit by a football? Do you know that being constantly targeted by you and your stupid football friends is getting old. You think it is funny, but I am enraged. It's been going on for so long. Stop calling me a fag, queen, quire and making fun of the way I dress. Stop the sexual gestures, as I pass in the hallways.

 The Victim

Dear Victim,

I am sorry for hitting you with the football. For me it was funny, but for you it probably made you angry at me. I am also sorry for bullying you in 5th grade. I am sorry my friends call you a fag and make sexual gestures when you pass us. They hear it from my dad all the time. We are just messing with you, it is really not a big deal. I am sorry.

The Bully

Update: During one of our programs, the bully opened up about this situation and wrote a letter to himself. Below is an extract from his letter.

Dear Bulldog,

I am alone, I am self-conscious, I am depressed. No one sees it, no one sees the real me. I have all these fake friends and I play football. I am being recruited by colleges, and all I am known for is football. But I don't care. I actually hate football. My dad forces me. He pushes and pushes me to be better. We run drills at home, I am on a strict high protein, low carb diet, I spend all my time studying plays, and watching football. I hate my life. My dad is fulfilling his dreams through me. I feel just disgusted. All I want to do is write. I love to write short stories, poems, and I read all the time. I want to be a writer.

I mention it and my dad goes off. He says that sissies write books and poems. I don't think he has ever read a book. He is a homophobe. He is aggressive and rough. I could never tell him that I am confused by my sexuality. He would disown me or probably kill me. I can't live like this anymore. I can't wait to get out of this town, away from him and football.

Dad does not know, but I applied to College so far away. I need to escape. I am so alone someone save me. My life is a total sham. I feel bad, now looking back at the kids I bullied, I only did it to look cool. I knew what to say because my dad bullies me. I knew how to attack them, I have been through it since 5th grade. Now in High School, I get to be the athlete with all the girls and I have to pretend that I love my life. I am ashamed.

High School Letter, 12th Grade: LGBTQ Bullying

Dear Bulldog,

I know why I ended up in this program with you. I am tagged as a troubled kid. I know I should not have made that scene in the cafeteria. I was tired of the bullying and the name-calling everyday from this punk. He is a homophobe! Quoting White Supremacy like lyrics to a song. He is a freak.

He would wait until after school with his nasty friends and their supped up cars and cat call me or whistle at me. Lizzie had to hold me back, I have a nasty temper and I would just yell back. Calling me fag, fairy, homo, and the list goes on.

Last summer, I saw him driving around my neighborhood trying to scare me as him and his stupid friends drove by my house shouting out bushtit. They would put their fists up and yell. It was annoying and him in his little clan does not scare me. I knew I could totally take him down.

One day, during our lunch period I just lost it and jumped across the table nailed him. I could not stop hitting him. He didn't even see it coming. I am not sorry for what I did, he stopped after that incident. I am sorry for getting caught and losing my temper in the dean's office.

I am so short tempered now, I have been bullied throughout middle school. When I entered high school, I was done with that crap, so that guy threw me over the edge. Thanks for teaching me how to manage my anger. I am learning a lot. I know I am tough on you guys sometimes.

Raging and Restless

Dear Raging and Restless,

Thanks for being in our group. I know the bullying was intense for you. You love to play the tough hard shell with me, but I know you must have been terrified. I'm so sorry that you had to go through all this to get it to stop. I know you refused to tell the deans, but you needed someone to advocate for you. What this boy did was more than bullying; he was harassing you and stalking you!

It breaks my heart to see you carry so much pain and anger, even after a year of working with us in this group. I have seen you, and you have so much energy and love to give. You hide it all away and wear your anger on your sleeve like a badge of honor. You are often volatile and really difficult to calm down if you escalate, because of the severity and longevity of the bullying and trauma you encountered. When you get angry, you just charge at people with your words and your fists. I have seen you pounce on people, and your emotion is one of pure rage. It's frightening. You told me, "I will never be that scared, frail little boy from middle school!"

I want to tell you that you aren't that boy. You're resilient, smart, funny, witty, caring, loving, loyal, and forgiving. I've seen you grow throughout our program, and I'm so proud of you. I would love it if you could work on your apologies and maybe try to let go of some of that resentment. I think you would feel lighter. You would finally feel free.

You will always have a special place in my heart. Don't ever stop being the fabulous, amazing you!

Sending you so much love and positivity,

The Bully Teacher

Stop and Think

Bullying and LGBTQ

In our programs, we have seen or heard about LGBT teens getting targeted and bullied in school. This targeting can lead to sexual assault and battery if things escalate. In these cases, fear seems to take the form of rage, and the bullying students have visceral reactions to someone's sexual identity or orientation. It can be terrifying.

Often out of fear, teens don't report this bullying. They are afraid of what might happen to them, or that things will escalate. When administrators or authorities don't jump in quickly enough and don't use the right strategies, things can easily escalate. We recommend having a respond-and-report process in place for any type of bullying, but especially for the LGBTQ students, as they are often violently targeted. It is good to have a safe place or community in school for the LGBTQ children.

Based on these two letters above, we have compiled strategies that parents can use immediately, to help navigate issues of sexual orientation, identity, and self-acceptance.

Strategies for parents and talking points for self-acceptance:

- We should help our children let go of what they can't change about themselves and focus on what makes them unique and strong. We can go back to using positive affirmations and building our child's confidence.

- We can ask our child, "What do you love about yourself?" "What makes you, you?" "How do you want to be seen?" "How can people show you respect and support?"
- We can discuss the fact that we are all unique—whether in terms of family life, school life, or friendships—and that our uniqueness adds to our lives. This discussion teaches children to understand that although there are things they can't change about themselves, they need to embrace and celebrate their differences.
- We can find support groups or organizations that will help us navigate these conversations and changes. We can give our children the support they need as they explore their sexual identity and orientation.
- We can get involved with the LGBTQ+ community. We can both join or attend events to meet people and learn more. You want your children to meet friends and build connections to feel supported, loved, and accepted.
- If our child is struggling with their sexuality, we can find a teen novel with characters who are struggling with this issue or a non-fiction book that deals with these topics. We should take the time to read the book that our child is reading. When we both finish, we can discuss how the book made them feel, what they found relatable, and what they wish we would understand. This discussion will help create a circle of open communication and trust with our child regarding this subject and what is happening in their life.
- We can watch LGBTQ shows, movies, or documentaries together, and talk about how they relate to our child's life. We can talk about the similarities and differences between the shows and our child's reality.
- We can learn the terms, definitions, and proper pronouns to show respect.
- We should ask which pronoun our child prefers and be open to expanding our vocabulary.
- We can ask questions and stay away from judgment. We should learn as much as we can about how our child feels and relates to others.
- We should repeat over and over again, "It doesn't matter who you date or love, or which gender you identify with. I love you unconditionally. I love all of you, and I am here."
- We can read a book, do our research, and educate ourselves.
- We should surround our family with people who support our child and their decision.
- We can ask our child how they want to come out or be introduced.
- We can talk about our child's anxiety or fears.
- We can find a parent support group to attend.
- We should love on our child and remind them every day why we adore them.

Discussing LGBTQ bullying can be a sensitive issue for our children, as they might also be figuring out their sexual identity or orientation. We should remember to be open and listen as our child talks about this subject or their experiences, and we should try to be as empathetic and understanding as we can be. We should stay away from stereotypes and judgments. The subject may be tough for our children to open up about, but once they do, we will have secured a new bond of trust and understanding with them.

Reflection Checkpoint

In this chapter, we encountered many different topics with multiple different strategies. It is time to bring all the information together. Middle and high school are tough. Youth are just starting to get a handle on who they are and to understand their emotions, all while navigating different social experiences. They experience so much change—in school, interests, and friends. They undergo the ups and downs of friendship, and through trial and error, they learn who their real friends are. Along with friendships, they dabble in romantic relationships. They learn how to treat someone and how they themselves should be treated. Social acceptance is important to them. When teens lack social and self-awareness, their behavior can turn negative. They can resort to a cycle of bullying, slut-shaming, rumors, and drama. When on the receiving side of this bullying and mean teasing, teens need strategies and tools to build resilience and bounce back from these negative attacks.

When looking for social acceptance, teens experience peer pressure. Some of them push the boundaries, with teasing, sexual identity, and experimentation (drugs, alcohol, sex, and sexual identity). And sometimes, when it all seems too much, we see the dangerous 3Ss (self-harm, suicide ideation, and self-hate). Even if the 3Ss are not present, stress and anxiety come to fruition for teenagers. This level of stress and anxiety is like nothing they have experienced before. They have more expectations from school, from the adults in their lives, and from themselves. All of these experiences can create problems under the surface. During this time, teens' self-esteem fluctuates due to insecurities about their physical characteristics, their social standing, and all of the experiences above. Teens understand the dimensions of conflict and sometimes hold onto their pain and trauma. These experiences are all so much to go through.

We find the best and most impactful strategy for working with this age group is having open conversations. Talking out their problems and our concerns makes the situation more tangible for them. Visualizing and processing situations can be very beneficial to them. They benefit from thinking about their current challenges, threats, or opportunities and from exploring possible solutions or outcomes. To open the lines of communication and create these powerful conversations, we have to create a safe space, a place where our children feel supported and loved, a place where there is no room for judgment or criticism. For educators and others who work with kids, creating a safe space is done through showing that we care and lending an unbiased ear. As parents, it is so much easier to establish this safe space early, in elementary school. Parents do need to be careful to define boundaries so that children still understand their jobs as parents. A kid who overshares with their parents can create an uncomfortable situation, and these youth usually do not have the same respect for their parents as others do. We want our children to handle situations on their own, but when they are really struggling, we want them to feel comfortable enough to come to us, regardless of what the issue is.

Youth have a hard time opening up, because they feel like there may be negative repercussions and they do not know how an adult might react. A good way to set up a high degree of trust is to offer a "no-questions-asked" pick-up. A no-questions-asked pick up is when a teenager calls a parent to pick them up, no matter where they are. This provides a way out for a youth, if they find themselves in a situation that makes them uncomfortable. We should continue to remind them that the pick-up is always an option. We can tell our child this for years, and they might not use the pick-up until their senior year in high school. We should be prepared that the pick-up could be from a party that we did not approve of them attending or a date gone awry. The fact is that they felt comfortable enough to call us—a noble choice. We should reward them by letting go and not bringing attention to the bad decision. We can reward ourselves, too. The pick-up is a big win for a parent; our child feels safe enough to let us in.

Dear Bully,
I forgive you.

Closing Remarks

We hope you enjoyed your journey through *Dear Bully*. Our wish is for you to better understand our lenses when it comes to bullying and social emotional learning. The book is based on our experiences and perceptions. We don't want to push our views onto you, as a reader. We want to expand your horizons to think differently about bullying.

We hope that the book moved you and expanded your thinking about the challenges our children face in school. For us, the process of writing was almost therapy, as we relived each story and remembered our encounters with each child. The book was an emotional release, and it gave us great joy to think about our children and how they have shaped our work as Bully Teachers. The book also got us to put our practices onto paper to share with you.

As Bully Teachers, we feel so much—empathy, sadness, anger, hopelessness, joy, and hope. At times, as Bully Teachers, we feel like we are on an emotional roller coaster. We cherish the bully letters where the child opens up and shares a glimpse into their world. We empathize with the victims as they share their painful memories and take their power back. During the process of writing this magical piece, we found ourselves drained. Some of the letters were dark, and they brought back troubling memories of working with some of the children. We were there with them through some of their darkest trials and tribulations. Some of the letters also brought up our own painful memories of being targeted, bullied, abused, neglected, harassed, made to feel unworthy, and actually having been the bully. Yes, we have all at some point bullied or stirred up drama. Bullying is a behavior, not a label. We hope this book will allow us to better understand each other and start eliminating the negative behaviors that fuel disconnection.

Sadly, some of our teens do not make it through the program, perhaps because of expulsion, moving, or dropping out or because their parents don't want them in group with us. The ones we lose are often the children who need the program the most. Children need more love, acceptance, and support. There is so much love to go around. We get so focused on productivity, goals, and tasks that we forget that love is the most important thing for us, as humans. Love drives us, creates us, and guides us. Our children need more love and less hate.

With all the bad and the ugly, there is always a light at the end of the tunnel. This book brought back the amazing memories that warmed our hearts and deepened our understanding of connection. We love to relive the stories of teens who kicked the habit, the toxic relationship, the trauma, the conflict. We love to talk about the children who are still in our programs and continually growing. We love to hear about the teens and young adults who, years later, still use the strategies and skills we taught them in our programs.

We are The Bully Teachers, and we love our work. We love to listen to children and make them feel heard and seen. We give them the tools to be kinder and wiser and to lead with compassion. These tools are not only for surviving school, but also for navigating through life.

Our work as parents and educators is never done. Exploring these stories and reading our children's deepest, darkest thoughts also drives us to do more work.

We hope this book provides you with more awareness about the issues and pressures our children face. We hope that throughout this book, we have shown that a bully is more than just a bully. A bully is a child who is in pain and suffering. Bullying is a silent cry for help. We are not born to hate; we are born to love. Our brains are wired to connect with others. By bridging the gap between the bully and the victim, we create hope.

By reading this book, you have opened new doors of communication with your child. Share your new discoveries with others and help us make this world a better place.

Sending Love and Positivity,

The Bully Teachers

If you have additional questions or want resources, please reach out to us on the Bulldog Solution website at www.bulldogsolutioninc.com

A special thanks to all my Bully Teachers. I am grateful for your work!

Michael Althouse	Marilyn Rodriguez
Leatha King	Nora Khani
Melissa Hasselbring	Susan Walters
Hannah Klint	Max Weiss
Ali Lueder	Amanda Madurski
Stacy Fredericks	Tamekeyo Griffin-House
Oriana Cristiani	Nick Setser
Bernard DeWet	Deandra Christianson
Bobby Hickson	Abbré McClain
Diana Mekarsky	Ellen Duong
Ed Caplain	Ari Smith
Tim Jauch	Gabrielle Flippo
Katrina Perry	Nosa Evomoyi
Harry Luk	Mary Adekale
Jennifer Thompson	Milissa Dooley - Embrey
Nadia Ismail	Ramah Smith
Chimare Eaglin	Angie Bozell
Chloe Broder	Amanda Beresford
Jamie Davis	Fithawit Berhe
Melissa Nuñez	Ayana Churn
Gianna Davis	Bruce Lines
Britney Thompson	Nancy Scott
Mary Grimm	Nosa Enomoyi
Joseph Marren	And many more...

Copyright © 2019 by Kortney Peagram

All rights reserved. No part of this book may be reproduced or used in any manner without written permission of the copyright owner except for the use of quotations in a book review. For more information, address: kortney@bulldogsolution.com

FIRST EDITION

www.bulldogsolutioninc.com

CPSIA information can be obtained
at www.ICGtesting.com
Printed in the USA
BVHW030301311219
568236BV00001B/217/P